How to Plan Your
DREAM
TRIP

Travel tips and digital
tools to plan for any
type of trip

HALI MOTLEY

This book is designed to save you so much time and money on the trip of your dreams! This is a collection of what I wish I knew when I started traveling. I've learned lots of ways to get discounts, skip lines, find the authentic side of cities, and make trip planning as painless as possible. I'd like to share all that with you, and MORE.

After traveling to 18+ countries and counting, this book shares everything that I wish I knew when I started so you can spend less time stressing and struggling, more time exploring and experiencing!

In this guide, I break down the complicated process of planning your DREAM TRIP into 6 manageable sections: **Who, What, When, Where, Why, and How.** We'll deep dive into how to plan, prepare, finance, and execute the trip of your dreams.

We'll go through steps of planning your trip with tips, tricks, explanations, advice, guidelines, and some embarrassing stories of my mistakes along the way.There are tons of links to explanations and important resources about traveling in today's world.

Hate the endless sea of dumb travel articles that promise to answer your questions but end up being some influencers packing list and photo gallery? Me too. This travel book is nothing like that.

Want to know if this book is right for you? Here's the Table of Contents to see for yourself.

- Create your want list
- The Who
  - Glass breaking
  - Types of travel partners
  - What to consider when choosing a travel companion
  - How to be a better travel companion
  - Personalities
  - Conflict Management
    - Don't go with Debbie Downer
  - Solo travel
  - Group Trips
  - Bonus games!
- The Where
  - Pictures vs reality
  - Underground vs super popular
  - Take advantage of the unexpected
  - Culture
    - Learning cultural norms and history
    - The Bathrooms
    - Culture Shock
- The When
  - Now is the time to make this happen
  - Factors to consider when researching when to travel
  - How long
  - Deeper dive into activities
- The How
  - Planning
    - How to break it down
    - FREE Travel Planner download
    - Planning with your traveling companion
    - Flights
      - Looking at flights
        - What you should consider before booking
      - Tips when booking flights
      - At the Airport
      - Going through security
      - General airport tips
      - General airplane tips
      - Airports in other countries
      - Ordering ride sharing services from the airport
      - General Q&A
    - Accommodation
      - Hotels
      - Airbnb

- - - Vrbo
    - Hostels
    - Couch Surfing
    - Resorts
    - Safety
    - Comparison Chart
  - Transportation
    - Subway/Metro
    - Trains
    - Buses
    - Boats / Ferry
    - Cars
    - Vans
      - Van Life advice
- Financing
  - How to save
    - guidelines
  - Mind tricks
  - How much to save
    - How much to budget for
    - The chart on some of my trip costs

- Preparing
  - Learning the language
  - Getting a passport
  - What to have physically printed
  - Currency
    - Exchange rates
    - How much cash you will need
    - Ordering or getting cash
    - Rule of thumbs for conversions
    - Sales tax vs VAT
    - How to store it
  - Time Change
  - Phone Services
  - Useful apps to have downloaded
  - Safety
    - Learn where the bad neighborhoods are
    - Someone else having your itinerary or location
    - Blending in and being aware
    - Self-protection moves
    - Apps for safety

Packing
    - Tips and guidelines

- My travel items that I love
- Picking out a hiking pack
- Final Thoughts
  - YOU CAN DO THIS.

Prologue

Who does this girl think she is?!

Great question! I'm Hali. I'm a 20 something-year-old business grad from rural Michigan. I'm a midwesterner who loves to read, paint, snuggle my cat, goof around with my friends, and of

course *travel.* I'm a hyperactive list maker, usually anxious mess, major clutz, certified goofball with no sense of style. My friends call me creative, but I think I'm just resourceful. I love keeping my friend group small and close-knit and my superpower is to create fun, random games out of anything. I'm not made of money, I have a desk job, I'm not a travel blogger, but I'm so excited to be able to help average Joes like me experience the world.

My Street Cred

I'm lucky enough to say that I've been to 18 countries (5 of them multiple times now) and 24 states + Puerto Rico. I've made more precious memories and taken more pictures while traveling than I could ever begin to describe and they mean the world to me.

Here's a list of the wild stuff I've been fortunate enough to do, just for a little inspiration:

- Swam under a waterfall in Puerto Rico
- Saw the Eiffel Tower twinkle at night with my mom in Paris
- Ate Fish and Chips in London
- Bar hopped for live music in Dublin
- Tried not to throw up in the Arctic Circle, Iceland
- Tried Trappist beers in Belgium (13% ABV, y'all. Dangerous)
- Wandered the gardens at Palace of Versailles
- Swished my feet around Loch Ness
- Presented a paper at Oxford University
- Spent 3 days snorkeling with sharks and turtles on a remote island in Malaysia
- Kayaked in a bioluminescent bay in Puerto Rico (shrimp jumped in our kayak)
- Play, fed, and swam with Elephants all day at an Elephant Sanctuary in Thailand
- Walked the Khaosan Road in Bangkok for street food and shops
- Salsa dance with strangers in San Juan, Puerto Rico
- Went to a Bar Crawl in Berlin for Halloween
- Hiked a glacier in Iceland without a coat on
- Cliff jumped at Odysseus's cave in Mljet, Croatia

- Swam in cave cenotes in Mexico with my boyfriend
- Cliff jumped 30m into the crystal blue cenote near Cancun, Mexico
- Snorkeled with manta rays and turtles in the Dominican Republic
- Tried to paddleboard in the Atlantic Ocean (fail, lol)
- Walked up Fushimi Inari in Kyoto, Japan
- Crossed the busiest street crossing in the world in Tokyo
- Went skydiving as soon as I turned 18
- Got an Airbnb with a rooftop infinity pool for less than $30 a night
- Wandered Park Guell in Barcelona
- Sat in on a private Flamenco dance in Madrid

Did you scoff and say to yourself, "yeah cool, but that'll never happen to me." And you're right! It will never happen *to* you. *You* have to make it happen. I've been in your shoes before, unsure of what to do or where to start, but here I am today with this incredible catalog of experiences. This book isn't about my adventures, it's about helping you pursue yours. It took a lot of determination to get the knowledge and experience to write this book; that's why it's a list of memories, not excuses.

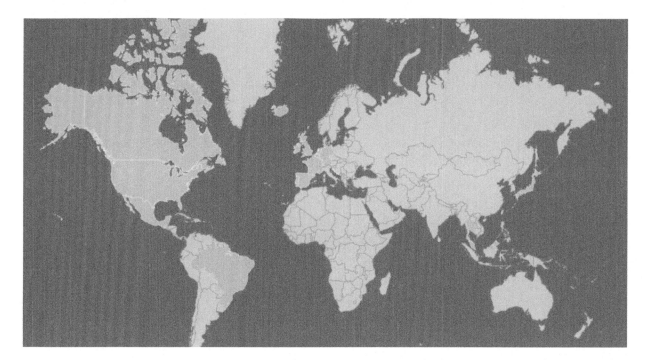

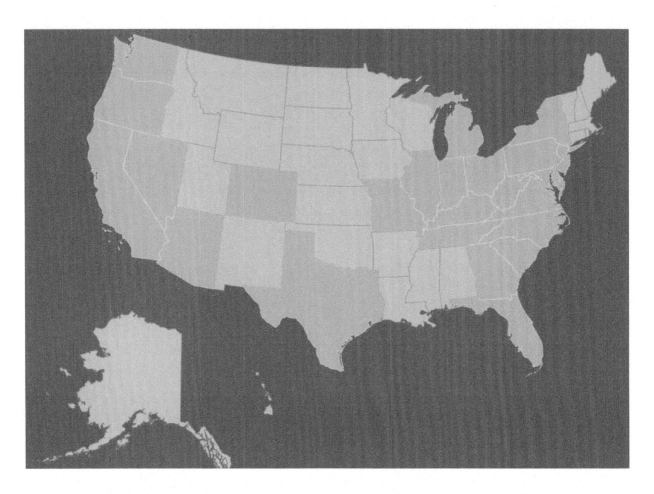

Why I'm writing this book

I'm writing this because traveling can seem extremely daunting with so many moving parts. I hope to inspire you to finally take all the steps of planning your big adventure and give you some added confidence to *actually go* make memories that you'll cherish forever.

I'm pretty good at breaking big concepts down into more manageable pieces so this is my attempt to take the complicated unknowns of planning a trip and make them approachable and manageable.

I have two goals: to inspire you to make your dream trip become reality and to walk you through the process of planning your trip. I've set up this book to try to accomplish both, but depending where you are in your personal journey, you might find more value in some chapters than others.

I'm not writing this to fill a word count requirement or to waste either of our time. You can trust that anything I've put in this book I've done so believing that it will add value. Please remember though, I'm like you! I don't have it all figured out. I can only pass on what I've learned, so there's a good chance that I won't have the answer to every question you have, but we can at least get started together.

Like your travels, your experience with this book is completely up to you. If you are chomping at the bit to get to all the details and tips of actually planning your trip, skip ahead and come back to this later. For those who bought this book in hopes of inspiration, start right here.

I'd love to encourage everyone to travel, but let's face it, traveling isn't for everyone. That's absolutely okay! I'm assuming that since you're reading this, you're interested in seeing more of this beautiful planet. I want to inspire you, push you towards your goals, help you figure out what it is you want your trip to be, help you avoid the mistakes that I made, and guide you through the daunting process of planning a trip!

However, there's only so much that I'll be able to do. I can give you insights and tips, but at the end of the day, I'm not responsible for making sure that you make this trip a reality --**you are.**

The only thing standing in your way is you.

DISCLAIMER:

I'm going to recommend a lot of planning ahead in this book, but I want to be clear that it's only to give yourself the most available options. I believe that knowledge is power.

So when I recommend looking into things, it's not to plan out every single minute of the trip. I recommend it so you can make the best choices for yourself to avoid major disruptions and allow you to have the best experience possible.

Enjoy the spontaneous adventures and use that knowledge to propel you forward, not hold you to a strict timeline.

There are so many benefits of seeing other parts of the world

In this book, I'm going to ask a lot of questions that only you'll know the answer to because they're all about you and your dreams. I want to start by highlighting some of the amazing things that we can all universally benefit from traveling. Let's be better people, shall we?

Here they are:

Practicing Empathy.

> Empathy requires Knowing that you Know nothing."
> —Leslie Jamison.

Empathy seems like one of those words that we think we know the meaning of. But do we?

Empathy - noun. The ability to understand and share the feelings of another.

When I was younger, when I thought of "having empathy" for someone, I thought of being kind to someone less fortunate than me. I don't like that as my first reaction because, now, I think that misses the point of empathy altogether. We should have empathy as often as we can for those around us as we ultimately face many of the same struggles: the need to belong, the need for security, the need for meaningful connection and purpose, the list goes on. It's not about bringing yourself down to someone's level when they're in a place of need, it's about taking all judgment out of your thoughts and trying to feel what others are going through, even for just a moment.

I believe that traveling to different parts of the world is such an important method of practicing empathy as we get to see and experience firsthand what others' lives are like. We get to see how different is not necessarily a bad thing and how much we truly have in common, no matter the language we speak or the culture we grew up in. Traveling is a means of keeping empathy at the forefront of our thoughts and adding much-needed perspective to our outlooks. Look, I can preach all day about this but the fact is we live kinder lives when we take a second to empathize with others. Empathy doesn't cost a thing yet adds so much value to life.

Dose of humility.
I'll be the first to admit that I take my wonderful life for granted all the time. Honestly, almost everyone in the western world does to some extent. I've never been so abruptly reminded of how fortunate and blessed I am then when traveling, especially to less fortunate nations. We get so caught up in our little quarles and upset over the simplest things like having to wait a day for our amazon package to arrive yet there are so many people going without food, water, shelter, medicine, education, security, freedom of will, let alone technology or surplus. We all need

something to knock us off our high horse sometimes and pop our bubble of ego. Travel will do that and then some. Trust me.

Embrace uncertainty.

We all handle uncertainty in different ways. Some of us can handle it pretty well most days, but others will struggle to get comfortable with not knowing how everything will happen. We can all think of a time in our lives that weighed heavily on our shoulders because we had to make decisions without knowing the benefits or consequences. A lot of high school seniors about to graduate experience this, with good reason! It's stressful, daunting, and can be draining, to say the least.

A lot of factors go into your capacity for uncertainty, you're not just good or bad at it. You're not a video game character that has a specific rating of how well you handle the unknown, however, similarly to a video game, you can "level up" your tolerance. I believe that the more comfortable we can become with uncertainty, the less stress we'll put on ourselves worrying about what may or may not happen.

So, if you follow my logic, then you might agree that the fastest way to "practice" this skill, is to expose yourself to it. Traveling, among many other things, is a great way to gain that comfortability and learn to roll with the punches. Traveling is filled to the brim with uncertainty. You can combat the unknown with research and planning, but no matter how much you do, there will always be situations that you do not expect or plan for. That's okay y'all, it's a good thing! Uncertainty is part of the excitement and thrill of exploring. You GET to find out what's around the corner.

Traveling can help you learn to stop viewing life as things happening to you and start viewing them as experiences that you get to live. We spend so much energy worrying about situations that might never happen that we miss opportunities to enjoy what is happening right in front of us. What I'm saying is that we're better off if we adjust ourselves to be more present in what's happening at the moment than agonizing over the future.

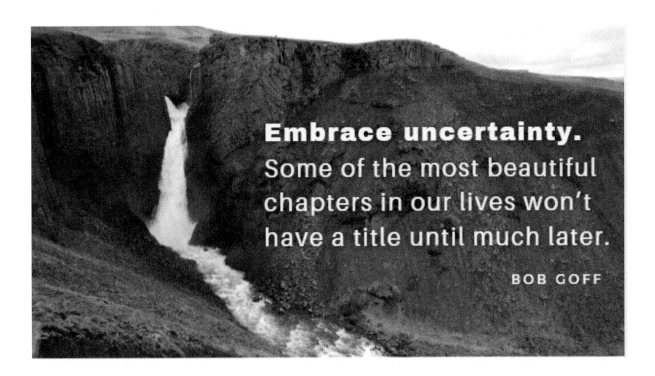

Embrace uncertainty. Some of the most beautiful chapters in our lives won't have a title until much later.

BOB GOFF

Storytime:

My (limited) capacity for uncertainty was a huge source of stress for me. If you feel stressed or anxious when thinking about the future, trust me, I've been right there with you. One of the most intense panic attacks I've ever had in my life was when I was in Iceland. I can still feel the tightness of my chest and the sharpness of my nails digging into my palms when I think back.

My travel buddy and I were driving our van through the Westfjords Region which was a series of gravel or dirt one-lane roads on the actual cliffside that kept going up and up into the fjords. Some serious white-knuckling driving conditions. Needless to say, it was not my choice activity of the day.

We would take turns driving and I didn't know what was worse: me being in control, hyper focused on the shrinking inches between the van and the cliffside, or her driving and me having to trust that she wasn't going to accidentally send us falling 45 stories down to our death. I'll skip the bit about having to pass a big truck coming in the opposite direction around a hairpin turn and get right to the panic attack. We had finally gotten to what seemed like the top of the mountain and were now in the middle of what looked like uncharted Martian terrain. No service, no road signs, no clear sense of if we were going the right way.

My nerves were shot and I couldn't stop obsessing about what we would do if we got a flat tire or if the engine failed. Cue my friend noticing me completely losing my shit and deciding to pull over. I launched myself out of the van and dropped to my knees in search of stability. The worries continued closing in. The ground was no help, so I stood up, started pacing, and counted to 20. I'm sure my friend was trying to comfort me, but honestly, I don't remember anything she said during that time. All I know is eventually I said to myself, "so what, Hali?". As soon as I asked myself that, I started to realize that I was so worried about something that hadn't even happened! "So what, Hali?"

So what? We had food and water for a few days. So what? We had a place to sleep in our van. So what? We were technically not lost since we were on the only road. So what? We had gas, there were no known predators. So what? Why was I so panicked?

I wasn't well-versed in coping with the unknown. I hadn't pushed myself to that limit before. In reaching a new "limit", I kept focusing on the bad things that might happen. I was so consumed with uncertainty that I didn't even see how beautiful and unique the scenery was around me. In that same area that same day, we stumbled on the most magical waterfall I've ever seen in my entire life. By confronting my capacity for uncertainty, I was able to clear my mind and open my eyes to the beauty of the present.

This is Dynjandi, meaning "Thunderous" (the top waterfall) because of its incredible sound from such a volume of water pouring down. It's over 30 stories high (330ft). I sat at the base of this waterfall for a long while and began to come to terms with my limited capacity for uncertainty. That moment of peace remains unrivaled in my mind. To this day, I still visit that memory when I need a "happy place" to calm down and relieve my anxieties. I had to face some hard truths about myself that day and I'm so thankful for it.

Facing your fears

Facing your fears has a ton in common with dealing with uncertainty, but it's worth focusing on each concept separately.

Facing your fears, like dealing with uncertainty, makes you come to terms with hard truths. It invites you to open your eyes and come to know what it is that makes your heart race, it compels you to empathize with yourself to uncover the core of your discomfort. It's a skill that we can improve on. It's a roadblock that we create, consciously or not, that we have to choose to get through.

 Fears are scary because they make us feel like we'll lose something. We'll lose our lives if we fall from someplace high, we'll lose an arm from a shark, we'll lose our friend if we move away. My favorite thing about facing your fears is looking at all the things you can gain. The more fears you face, the more confident you become in yourself, the more courage that you prove to yourself that you have, the more badass stories you can tell. The more experiences you can have in life.

You gain more examples to look back and say "if I could do that really scary thing, then I can surely do this". It can snowball into all aspects of your life. Facing a fear of heights for example could give you the confidence to look back and say -If I could stand in the glass box at the top of the Sears Tower in Chicago (110 stories high), then I can have the courage to tell a loved one something hard but important to say. Or apply for the job that's a long shot. Or move to the city you want to go to. So change your perspective on fear, because:

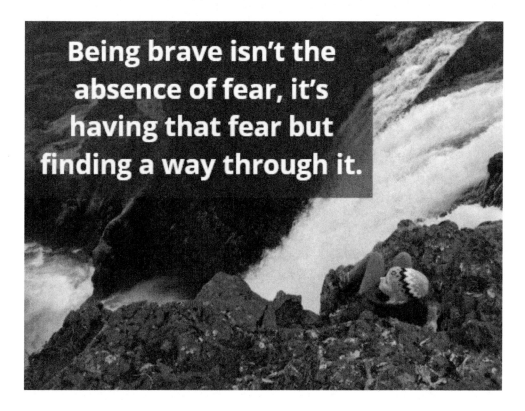

Being brave isn't the absence of fear, it's having that fear but finding a way through it.

Push your comfort zones.
"Don't find yourself, Accept yourself."

I love that quote. We get bombarded with advertisements that claim to have just the thing we need to make our lives better. To make us feel better. To help us try to feel like someone else. We hear about people who travel to "find themselves". I'll admit, that's part of the appeal traveling initially had for me too.

But what I've learned is that I didn't find myself in any place that I went, but I did start to accept what I did and didn't enjoy: foods, activities, outfits, personality types, topics, conversations, etc. I started to accept what I cared more about, and by default, I began to let go of what I didn't truly care about. I began to accept what my gut was telling me and started to ignore what those advertisements told me I should be. I hope the same for you, whether you find that through travel or other experiences. Accepting yourself, like most journeys worthwhile, isn't going to happen over night. Paired with a lifetime of trial and error, traveling can help show you the way to self-acceptance.

We get to make choices everyday that determine whether we continue where we are with what we have, or push us to dream bigger and grow a little more. I imagine a little tiny seed that's cozy in it's natural shell, but full of potential to flourish, to grow into a beautiful plant. Maybe it's a plant that creates gorgeous flowers or even better, avocados! You can be an avocado (yum!).

Communication skills improve.
Traveling will help you improve your ability to express and communicate your intentions. Sure, you might pick up some handy phrases while you're travelling, but you'll also become more emotionally intelligent through a better understanding of facial expressions, hand gestures, general body language and stances, etc. It may not feel like your communication skills are improving as you flail your arms emphatically at the street vendor, gesturing excitedly for a croissant but receiving instead a mystery meat tart, but these are necessary growing pains. The good news is you'll be practicing (and improving) your communication skills all the time without even realising it. Soon you'll be experiencing the great pride of walking home from shopping at the quaint French market, realizing you effortlessly had an entire 60 seconds of conversations about grapes (take that, croissant-turned-meat tart!) with an equally quaint grandma-aged fellow shopper.

You'll also get better at piecing together context clues to get the meaning of what someone is saying when you can't understand every word. Traveling can even help you get used to thinking and responding quicker since you'll have to process a lot of information very quickly, whether that be listening, reading or navigating. Sound like a mental overload? You can do it. And you'll be able to better empathize with speakers of other languages who go through the same process. I narrate life to myself all the time to make sense of what's going on around me and I like to imagine a world where we are all well-equipped to express and understand each other for the benefit of sharing our stories (and bad puns!).

Another Traveler's Advice

I have spent hundreds (dare I say thousands?!) of hours reading blog posts by other travelers, always on the lookout for new tips and tricks of the trade. In many ways, those hours spent reading blog posts inspired me to gather my experiences, and everything I learned from others along the way, to share in one collective how-to book. There's a sense of community among travelers, and even if you haven't taken your dream trip yet, there are plenty of ways to tap into that community to find inspiration to get started. As a "welcome to the neighborhood", I want to introduce you to Shalee of Shalee Wanders, a fellow Michigan native with an appetite for adventure. When I was in the process of planning for my first big trip, I came across Shalee's travels and her hilarious-inspiring-relatable-all-of-the-above blog, Shaleewanders.com. Her words were just what the doctor ordered to help me feel like making the trip of *my* dreams happen was well-within my reach.

Now, dear reader and travel neighbor, as we take a deep breath and prepare to jump into the planning process together, let's kick-off with some wise words from Shalee herself:

"When I initially began traveling, I'd fill my trunk to the brim with as much as it could hold – tents, towels, sleeping bags, pillow, expired snack bars, and more bug spray than I would ever need. I didn't travel far, mostly within a few hours of my home in mid-Michigan, but it opened a world of possibilities.

As I grew my travels expanded, from the shores of the Great Lakes to the oceanic boundaries and, eventually, to over 35 countries. The thing about travel is that it's evolutionary. You start somewhere. It doesn't have to be across the world. Sometimes it's just our backyard. Finding beauty close to home is sometimes our greatest inspiration.

Just because you haven't made it to Europe, or Mexico, or Hawaii, or Florida, doesn't mean you aren't a traveler. Like us, trips are made in all shapes and sizes. **Instead of focusing on all the places you haven't been, be proud of all the places you've gone."**

Thanks, Shalee!

@shaleewanders

WHO, WHAT, WHEN, WHERE, WHY, AND HOW

This book is here to help guide and manage your travel-related expectations. I'll be honest, I have a hard time bouncing back from being disappointed by my expectations, both with travel and in my everyday life. Left unmanaged, expectations can become your worst enemy. The good news is that there are skills and processes you can practice to find the middle ground between hoping for the best and expecting the worst when planning your dream trip. Let's get started with a deep dive of the basic considerations when planning your trip: who, what, when, where, why, and how.

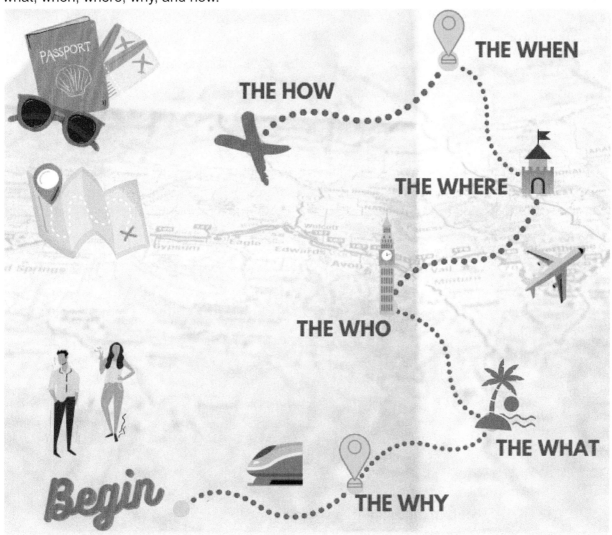

I'm going to go against the catchy way to say those and rearrange the order a bit. Grab your ticket for The Why, What, Who, Where, When, How Express!

First, boarding at the station, we will explore *The Why*. I believe that first identifying and understanding your desire for travel is essential.   Once you have the answer to your "why", the rest will fall into place.

Then we'll take a train ride at *The What* to reflect on what it is that you enjoy doing and what type of trips there are for the taking.

Chugging along, next up is *The Who* where you'll explore who you want to spend all this time with while traveling on your dream trip.

 As we approach *The Where, don't forget to look out the window with eyes wide to a world of wondrous destinations.*

After breathing in the fresh air-of-possibilities at The Where, we're off to *The Whe*n to find the best time of the year to visit your dream destination and make sure we pencil it in on your calendar.

We end our ride at *The How,* but for you, your journey is just beginning. Before we go our separate ways, we'll get organized and make sure you have money in your pocket, accommodations set, and modes of transportation booked.

While why, what, who, where, when, how doesn't roll off the tongue quite as easily, approaching things in this order will make planning your trip easier and help you better understand what to expect. Your one ride away from everything you need to make your dream trip a reality. Choo choo, all aboard!

ACTION ITEM CHECKLIST

1 THE WHY Motivations
- Think about what fuels you and this dream trip
- Enjoy your motivating tasks to get pumped up!
- Acknowledge and accept your travel fears
- Day dream about your trip = visualization

2 THE WHAT Activities
- Daydream about your "perfect" day and night related to traveling, things you'd love to do
- Research the activities that come to mind to make sure they're a good fit for you
- Create your want list

3 THE WHO Companions
- Decide on traveling companions (if not yet determined)
- Talk with companions about their wants, don't wants and expectations
- Find common interests and split up planning duties

4 THE WHERE Destinations
- Research the best locations to do the activities you and your travel companion(s) are interested in
- Decide where you're going!
- Begin looking at logistics of getting there (preliminary planning)

5 THE WHEN Timelines
- Research destination for ideal times to go and weather conditions for your preferred time of travel
- Establish a window of opportunity to travel with your companion(s)
- Begin hammering our details of when you're going!

6 THE HOW Details
- Begin putting a tentative plan together with companion(s)
- Book activities, accommodations, transportation, and making preparations for trip
- Finalize details and get ready for your dream trip!

THE WHY

The Why

This chapter is all about figuring out your motivations. The more you know about yourself (what your strengths are, what gets you excited, what you prefer to avoid at all costs), the easier it will be to make decisions during the planning process to create a trip you can really get excited about. Being in tune with why you want to travel will provide you with a reservoir of inspiration to tap into when you need a little extra push to stay on course. The more you know about yourself and what you dream about → the more clearly you can *see* your dreams → the much more likely that you'll *make* them come true.

I won't lie to you. This first chapter is going to be the hardest to navigate. It requires looking inwardly to understand your true feelings, not what social media and external influences tell you to want. Get real with yourself. Sit down and take the time to daydream, let your mind wander. Think about what you would do if there were no obstacles: no (reasonable) money restraints, no requesting time off work, no opinions of others, no fear, no nagging sense of responsibility. Of course, we shouldn't just run away from everything we're responsible for, but that's why daydreaming is a perfect way to start getting comfortable with thinking about what you want from life!

Daydreaming helps us see what we want our lives to look like so we can see what changes could be made from our current status. I'm making the argument that it's okay to be selfish sometimes for what you *truly care about.* Not whims or impulses. You know why? Because when we realize our dreams, pursue them, and put in the hard work of accomplishing them, we become better versions of ourselves. We become more fulfilled, and as a result, we have more happiness and joy to pass onto others around us.

Think about it, would you rather be around someone who is outspokenly discontent with their life or someone who is energized by their passions?

That someone is you, and you get to choose which someone you want to be.

Getting Motivated

<u>Difficult goals require strong motivations</u>

Let's paint the scene. It's a Tuesday morning in Paris. You wake up the day after your flight and it's your first full day to go see the city and the Eiffel Tower. You walk over to the window and open the cream colored shutters to let in the smell of fresh bread from the boulangerie two shops down and the soft sounds of people making their way down the street. You see a cute cafe just beginning to put the chairs outside and take in the historic charm of the architecture around you from your second floor view. You hear a vespa wiz by and the light breeze isn't what gives you the goosebumps, it's the sudden moment when it officially hits you. YOU ARE IN PARIS.

Do I have you hooked? Did that get you excited? Hold onto that feeling because it's going to take strong motivation to get you through the hard work and dedication it takes to budget, save for, plan, and execute a big trip. It takes a lot of sacrifices to make traveling a reality, and it's inevitably going to be difficult some days. Saving hundreds or thousands of dollars doesn't happen by accident and it's not easy. Putting in the hours to research and plan and make reservations can be exhausting. Choosing to stay in while your friends go out for dinner and drinks can be painful.

The clearer your "why" is to you → the easier it will be to stay motivated→ to save that money and put in the hours → the sooner you'll be able to make those dreams come true.

I like watching motivational videos, but what gets you motivated?

Talking with your friends?
Painting, writing, creating?
Going for a run or dancing?
Making boards on Pinterest?
Reading your favorite travel blog?
Is it looking at amazing travel photos?
Watching a great movie that gets you feeling good?

Life is more fun when we feel motivated, it's easier to tackle that to-do list, to do that chore you've been putting off, to break out of your daily routine, to finally begin working toward your goals.

So while we get a better idea of what your travel Why is, I recommend you do whatever it is that gets you motivated! Get excited, get cheery, get smiley! Let's make this as fun as possible because getting started is always the hardest part. Let's jump that hurdle and launch into motivation exploration!

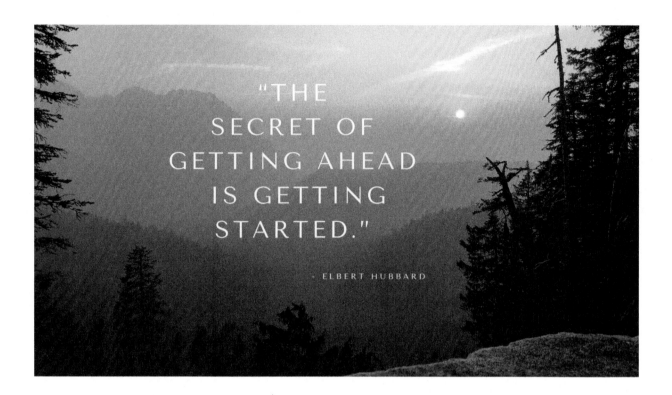

"THE SECRET OF GETTING AHEAD IS GETTING STARTED."

- ELBERT HUBBARD

<u>What created this dream?</u>
So you want to travel. Why?

Do you know? Can you say why in one sentence?

You didn't buy this book to learn how to book a girls' weekend in Nashville. I'm guessing you bought this book for either a big trip or to learn about tips for traveling often. You bought this because you dream big. If you have a hard time summarizing why you want to travel into a sentence or two, then let's ask more questions! It's totally fine to not be able to put your Why into words right now, don't worry, we'll work on figuring it out together. We've got more exercises to help bring clarity.

<u>Figuring out where this dream was born might help</u>
Ask yourself these questions to get thinking about what piqued your interest and maybe your why will become more clear.

> What created this dream in your mind?
> What was the trigger? What sparked it for you?
> Was there a single event that caused it?
> Was it a picture that sparked your interest?
> Was there someone in your life who told a story that inspired you?

Was it an event that you heard about that you thought would be awesome?
Did you go somewhere and discovered you were hooked from that point?
Did you read a book set abroad that stole your heart and you had to see it in person?

Anything make a memory appear in your mind's eye? Let's try it from a different angle.

What fuels you?
For me, I'm obsessed with the concept of time. I'm unhealthily aware that I only have a limited time, so my fuel comes from wanting to make the most of the time that I do have.

I love spending my time searching for the best ice cream spots, getting water up my nose from crashing waves, acting like morons with my best friend wherever we go, and super gluing googly eyes on random items with my boyfriend.

What fuels you?

Ask yourself these questions to get thinking about what gets you excited, motivated, or overall jazzed up.

Are you always looking to try new restaurants?
Are you intrigued by different languages?
Do you like to strike up conversations with strangers?
Do you like to watch or read things about different cultures or ways of living?
Are you fascinated by fashion and different appearances?
Are you into extreme sports? Are you an adrenaline junkie?
Do you love to hike? Maybe you love to run or bike?
Do you have a bucket list? Have you checked anything off? If so, what?
Are you obsessed with the ocean or being in/by/on the water?
Do you love the feeling of flying? Do you love the view from an airplane window?
Do you crave a different climate than the one you live in?

Did anything pique your interest? Make you stop and think for a second? Explore those. Think of your own. Think about the memories that got your heart pumping and you wanted to brag about. Follow that path.

Overcoming Fears

Why haven't you planned this trip yet?

Let's switch gears for a minute. Maybe you *just know* deep down that traveling is something that you want to do. Or maybe you've already figured out your "why". Fantastic. I do have one question though.

WHY haven't you planned this trip yet?

That's a biggie, isn't it? I know there are plenty of practical and justifiable reasons why we have to stay put for a while. I acknowledge them, I know them well, I live with them too. But let's not confuse the reasons why you **can't** with the reasons why you **haven't.**

Let's address some fears that keep people from making the trip to wonderland. Business nerds like me refer to these Barriers to Entry, aka the things that hold us back.

It's scary.

Validation:

It IS scary! Like I mentioned before, there's a ton of uncertainty involved in traveling, it's really daunting. It feels overwhelming to think about actually making it happen. There's no way to look into the future to see that everything will be alright or that it will even be worth it. I've booked so many flights with the 'fluttery butterflies in my stomach' feeling. I've stared at the "confirm purchase" button for 3 minutes before clicking it more than once. My hands get shaky and I find it physically impossible to stop my leg from bouncing more than I'd like to admit.

Rebuttal:

It's totally normal to feel that way! There's nothing wrong with being nervous or afraid, but is that a good enough reason to keep you from all the good that can come out of going? The memories, laughs, experiences, foods, views. If it's scary, that means there's room to grow. It's up to you to view this either as an impossible task or as a worthwhile challenge. Just imagine how much more confidence you can have once you come back as a newly experienced traveler.

*"If you are pained by any external thing, it is not this thing
that disturbs you,
but your own judgment about it.
And it is in your power to wipe out this judgment now."
— Marcus Aurelius*

*"We are more often frightened than hurt, and we suffer
more in imagination than in reality."
— Seneca*

Scrolling is just easier.

Validation:

No brainer here, it's so much easier to just scroll Instagram to see endless gorgeous views and get a glimpse of gorgeous spots. Of course it's easier, you just click on the app and let it do the work for you.

Rebuttal:

Scrolling is just viewing, it isn't *experiencing.* "You're not tasting the cooling creaminess of a pina colada as the glass gently condensates in your hand. You're not swinging your hips and shaking your hair to the beat of a live salsa band. You're not feeling the sun's healing rays kiss your skin as you meander through cobblestone streets, blissfully unaware of the time." Unfortunately, those memories aren't your memories, at least not yet.

*"It never ceases to amaze me: we all love ourselves more
than other people, but care more about their opinion than
our own."
— Marcus Aurelius*

It's hard to sacrifice other fun

Validation:

Ooof, this one was a toughie for me. Traveling requires sacrifice *now* in order to go *later*. That's so hard to recognize. It's even harder to actively choose NOT to do something fun today with your peeps in order to save the money or vacation time. It's hard to miss out on that new movie or Sunday brunch or ice cream. It's hard to pick up shifts to make some cash. It's hard to tell your friends or family no, you're not coming with them. It's hard not to use that free day to do something else other than planning. It's hard to put in the time to make this trip happen. I get it, it's just *hard* sometimes.

Rebuttal:

IT. IS. WORTH. IT. Put things into perspective, when you look back on the year, or this decade, or your life will you remember going out to eat for dinner down the street or getting dinner in that new place on your big trip? It's easy to do what's comfortable or convenient, but that's not usually what ends up being memorable.

> "A gem cannot be polished without friction,
> nor a man perfected without trials."
> — Seneca

There's never a right time

Validation:

To quote the wise song *All Star*, "Well the years start coming and they don't stop coming". Ya got that right, Smash Mouth. Time is going to pass whether we like it or not, but wow, it flies by. We've always got something going on, don't we? Have to go to school, have to work, have to be present for our family, be at that special event that's coming up. It's not easy to set time aside, it's not easy to ask your boss for time off, it's not easy to figure out family logistics. It's not easy to accept that life will go on without us while we're away.

Rebuttal:

However, We *could* all use a little change (more *All Star* lyrics, I'm not sorry). As much as I wish we could pause time, we can't. We can't be in two places at once. You bought this book because you want to travel, so you need to make the time to travel. I'm not saying find the time, because you'll probably be looking for a long time. Make the time.

Everything will be fine while you're gone, nothing will crash and burn, it'll be okay. No better time than the present.

> *"While we wait for life, life passes."*
> — Seneca

Don't have enough experience

Validation:

Sometimes it feels like so many people know what they're doing and we don't. We don't know where to even start or what to look up. Sometimes we tell ourselves we could do it if only we had someone to show us the ropes, but we don't. Our minds sometimes default to the thought "but I don't know how to do that", and we don't challenge that thought.

Rebuttal:

We'll never know everything we need to know, we can only make the best of what we have and strive to keep learning more. There's not some imaginary test that you have to pass to get started or a certain point where you're suddenly "experienced" enough to begin. We all start with no experience and gain it along the way. Don't let that negative Nancy in your mind keep you down, get started and you'll learn as you go. You'll make mistakes, sure, but so what? Take them as lessons learned and know that we all make mistakes. (I wrote this book so you can learn from mine!)

> *"Nobody can go back and start a new beginning, but anyone can start today and make a new ending."*
> — Maria Robinson

Too many of us are not living our dreams because we are living our fears.
– Les Brown

"Didn't make sense not to live for fun
Your brain gets smart but your head gets dumb
So much to do, so much to see
So what's wrong with taking the back streets?
You'll never know if you don't go (go!)
You'll never shine if you don't glow"

All Star - Smash Mouth

KEY TAKEAWAYS OF THE WHY

- Find your powerful motivations that will keep you going.
- Daydream about what you would really love to spend your time on.
- Think about what fuels you and follow that feeling.
- Fear is natural, but you can choose to overcome those fears.

THE WHY
Motivations

- Think about what fuels you and this dream trip
- Enjoy your motivating tasks to get pumped up!
- Acknowledge and accept your travel fears
- Day dream about your trip = visualization

THE WHAT

Do what you actually enjoy doing with your days. Forget the rest.

Remember how I reorganized the Who, What, When, Where, Why? It's important to note that I'm asking you WHAT you want to do before I'm asking you WHERE you want to go. We need to figure out what you enjoy before you can decide on the best place to do it.

Most of us don't have a ton of money or time to spend on traveling, so I want to help you make the most of your trip by aligning it to your desires as much as possible.

If you haven't asked yourself lately, allow me the honor of asking: What do you want to do today?

What a simple question. I remember asking myself that all the time when I woke up during Summer Break when I was a kid, but I can't remember the last time I asked myself that as an adult. I still ask myself questions on my days off, but they're more like "What do I need to get done today?" "What do I have scheduled today?" "When do I have to meet so-and-so?" and of course, the never ending "What should I make for dinner?".

When did I stop asking myself what I **want** to do today? I have no idea, but I do believe that life's too short to get stuck in the same old dull routine. So we're going to do something about it. We know that you want to travel and you're working on figuring out your motivations, aka WHY you want to travel. Now let's figure out what you want to do while you travel!

Let's start asking ourselves what we **want** to do again.

If you could do anything today, what would you do?

Would you want to go to the beach? Scuba dive? Go skiing? Hike a mountain to watch the sunrise? Try a bunch of European cafes? Explore a castle? Go deep sea fishing?

Let's daydream! You have to really commit to it. Sit or lay down, close your eyes, let your mind wander through all the possibilities that you find interesting or fun. Listen to Live like you were dying by Tim McGraw if you need to.

Did you come up with something? Great! If not, we'll get there!

Not everyone can come up with just one thing, I get it. I always have trouble picking *one* favorite song. If you can't hone in on one dream activity, start by writing down everything that comes to mind and then pick your top 3!

Hold onto those daydreams and fill in as many details as you can about what you want that day to look like.

What's the first thing you want to do in the morning? Go get breakfast somewhere overlooking a view? Sleep in until you're ready to get moving around? Start with a leisurely walk? Now start thinking about the main events, the thing you thought about first, fill in what the day looks like around that and keep going into the night, what will you do after? Go out for a quaint dinner? Find a high energy place to enjoy the atmosphere? Find a spot to sit and enjoy some sounds of nature like crickets chirping or waves rolling on the sand?

Here's my first piece of advice for this section.

Use this exercise to try to dig deep to the root of what you want to do so you can plan your trip around that. It's easy to fall into the idea that you want to go to a certain place because the idea of it is so romantic or exciting or novel. Maybe you got the idea a long time ago and you haven't stopped to ask if that's what you want today verus what you wanted years ago. It's okay if what you wanted in the past is no longer what you want right now.

If you said something like "I've always wanted to go to Scotland since I was little!" then by all means, look into going to Scotland, but just be sure to look at it through the eyes of who you are today and the reality of the activities you were excited about as a kid.

Here's an example: Let's say you watched a very cool movie when you were a kid and decided that one day you would explore Scottish Castles (Any Harry Potter fans have that fantasy a lot?) because you loved the idea of running around playing out the movie scenes. Maybe Scotland has continued to stick around in your mind because of that but you've long since forgotten about playing out the movie scenes.

All I'm suggesting is that you take a step back and ask "Am I still excited by the idea of exploring castles in Scotland, willing to either drive or join a tour bus that will take me from sight to sight?" If the answer is yes, then book that tour and buy the tickets! But if you're not so sure a day on a bus looking at beautiful ruins is for you anymore, that's where you start asking yourself what you'd *actually* want to do. Maybe what you'd like to do is not far from that original idea. Maybe you'd rather stay in Edinburgh, walking the streets, exploring the pubs and live music, seeing plays or shows, going on a haunted ghost underground tour. Maybe it's completely different now and you'd rather spend your vacation on a sunny beach.

Make sure the trip is what you need right now.

Our wants and needs change as we grow and experience more, go through different chapters in our lives. That's part of the human experience, evolving. Think of our ideas like software that needs periodic updates. Be sure to check in with who you are right now and what your needs are, not just defaulting to what you had thought you would like before.

Here are some factors to consider that might help figure out your needs.

Energy Level - Are you looking for a high-energy environment with a lot of excitement and moving parts or more low energy, simple relaxation?
Think: Bustling Asian food market vs. hammock by the beach.

Amount of Transportation - Are you looking to explore a sample platter of multiple cities and/or countries or do you prefer to get settled in one place for a thorough experience of all the activities?
Think: European culture tour vs. getaway at a resort in Costa Rica.

Physical exertion - Are you looking to push your body and mind to new heights or relax and slow down for a while?
Think: Training and finally climbing Mt Kilimanjaro vs. light exploring areas by foot with an easy going picnic lunch.

Maybe you've been going a mile a minute juggling work, school, relationships, home life, etc., and need to slow down for a while. Maybe you've been stuck in a rut and want something new, bold, and exciting to look forward to. Knowing yourself, your current needs and wants, will help you get the most enjoyment out of your trip.
The list of amazing places to see on our gorgeous planet. I definitely have some personal favorites, but this book isn't about prescribing "The Top 5 Places You Absolutely Must See Before You Die Because Somebody Else Said So". I want to help you explore your options and pick what's right for you!I won't list everything (and realistically can't ... hello, "marvelously endless"), I can point you in the right direction using this handy chart of general trip types.

General types of trips

Type of Trip	Cost	Prep Work	Customizability
Resorts	Medium - High	Very Low	Low
Cruises	Medium	Very Low	Low - Medium
Explore a city	Low	Low	High
Tour cities in one country	Low-Medium	Medium	High
Tour of multiple neighboring countries	Medium - High	High	High
Roadtrip	Low-Medium	Medium- High	Very High
Camping/hiking	Low - Medium	Medium- High	High
Guided tours	Medium - High	Low	Very Low

Think about your needs and wants, your finances, the amount of planning you want to do ahead of time, and how much flexibility you want to have while you're actually there. After consulting the chart, does it match up with the trip type you had in mind? Does it match up with your daydream activities? Don't be afraid to go through a few rounds of reflecting and reconsidering to make sure your trip will check all the boxes while accommodating your needs.

Dam Square in Amsterdam, The Netherlands

How to decide WHAT to do

Simply put, researching is the best way to decide **what** to do.

Now that you have your wants and needs, daydream activities, and type of trip in mind you can start doing some research to get a sense of what that looks like in reality. Pinterest and Google are great starting points with loads of resources and reviews. Sites like Groupon and Tripadvisor will help you make sense of what's possible to take on during different trip durations and budgets (more on that later!). Knowing what all will be involved (and sometimes required) to make your dream activity happen will help you decide if it truly matches your expectations and will still be the right fit for you.

For example, if your daydream involves snorkeling on the coast of an island, then look for the best snorkeling spots and go from there. Read about what the tours involve, what's included, and if you're sold on that activity and all that goes with it (being on the beach, riding on a boat, swimming in open saltwater, etc.), then great! If you decide that maybe that activity isn't what you had in mind, go back to daydreaming.

It's okay if the idea you had in mind isn't what you end up going with --that's the beauty of daydreaming in the age of the internet! Just like when you're scouting for which product is the best fit for you on Amazon, you can use the descriptions and feedback from others to decide if you're on board with all aspects of the dream activity you have in mind. The bus ride to the beach was so twisty-turny that several people left reviews saying they got carsick? Well, now you know. Take the time now to weigh out what gets you excited and what prompts you to reconsider.

Let me explain a bit more about my logic behind deciding if an activity is going to be a good fit by setting a scene. Your dream activity is seeing your favorite European football team play at their home stadium in person. You think "Great, I already *know* what I want to do, easy." So you start by booking other details of your trip first, let's say it's a lavish hotel suite in the city center. You realize too late that not only is the stadium actually farther out from the city center than you thought, but there are no longer tickets available for the match you planned on attending, and even if there was, your fancy suite drained your budget leaving you unable to afford a ticket anyway.

It's so easy to look at Airbnbs, hostels, and hotels and want to pay higher prices because it looks nicer or has more perks. At the end of the day, you have to think about what's more important to you. Is it the view from your top floor suite? Or giving up the view for a cheaper place to be able to afford a ticket to see your favorite team play? Treat your desires like the priorities that they are, put them first. Let everything fall into place after.

Making decisions about what you want to do before looking into what all it entails is like being at a restaurant and ordering from a menu without descriptions of the food. You thought you really wanted that chicken sandwich, but turns out it's piled high with onions AND tomatoes (your two arch nemesis in the food world) and comes with a side of coleslaw instead of fries (come on, everyone knows fries >>>>> coleslaw)! You're left fry-less, hungry, and out of money for a new meal. You have to ask the right questions to make sure you know what you're getting into before you commit to an experience that's not what you were expecting. You could have easily asked for no tomatoes or onions, possibly substituted fries for coleslaw, or picked an entirely different meal (you were also eyeing the pasta anyway) if only you had asked what came with the meal you were ordering. Bottom line is, do your daydreaming and your research to make sure you don't get stuck with onions, tomatoes, and coleslaw on your trip.

Do some digging and start building your want list. Not your wish list, because that means it's just a pipeline. This is your want list, like what you want right now and what you plan on making happen.

We'll talk later in The How about organizing your thoughts, links, resources, and findings. For now, feel free to just open up a document of your choice and dump it all in there as you start.

Be sure to give your computer a proper warning about what it's about to endure, because I've never in my life been able to look at trip planning stuff without having 6+ tabs open at all times. Sorry computer, I love you!

KEY TAKEAWAYS OF THE WHAT

- Daydream and figure out what you actually want to do while you travel, then base the trip off those activities. Basically, try to figure out what you want to do before where you want to do it
- Know what you're getting into and what your priorities are
- Ask yourself what you need in a trip right now, not what you had imagined previously
- It's okay if what you wanted in the past is no longer what you want right now.

2 THE WHAT Activities

- Daydream about your "perfect" day and night related to traveling, things you'd love to do
- Research the activities that come to mind to make sure they're a good fit for you
- Create your want list

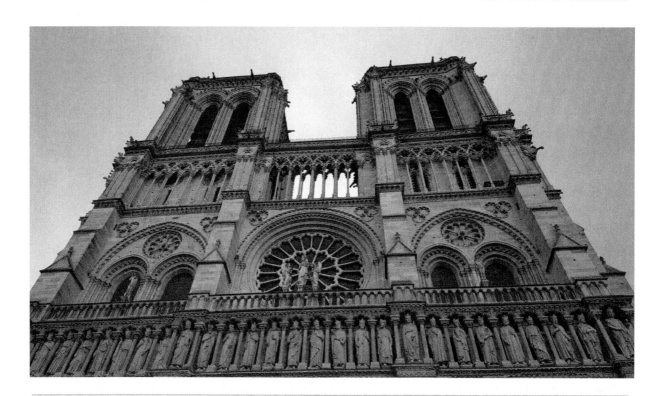

THE WHO

Who you travel with will affect your trip. Choose wisely.

Now that you have an idea of what you want to do, you get to decide who you want to ride shotgun! Sometimes you'll know who you are bringing along for your adventure right from the start. However, in general I recommend honing in on what it is YOU want to experience before sending out invites to potential travel pals. Ideally you and your travel buddy will be on the same page about your main desires and will be ready and willing to compromise on the rest. Speaking of which…

GLASS BREAKING

Okay, y'all. Here's the part where I burst your bubble of any and all romantic notions that traveling with someone is going to be "just like in the movies" with a montage of endless laughter and a guaranteed musical number perfectly suited for frolicking into the sunset. NOPE. *glass shatter sound effect*

Strap in for a roller coaster ride of emotions throughout the trip regardless of who you're traveling with. There will likely be moments of frustration and miscommunication, maybe even some hurt feelings after a stressed induced bickerment (the lovechild between bickering and arguments). You're not always going to be in the mood for the same activity, have the same preference on which restaurant to eat at, or agree that you're going the right direction to get back to your accommodation after an already long day of walking. That glass I just shattered? Toss the unrealistic expectation that nothing will require deliberation or compromise right out that window. Like I mentioned before, I am writing this book to help manage your expectations and set you up for planning a successful trip. Nobody is amazing to be around 100% of the time, not even you. We all have different triggers that make us anxious, annoyed, stressed, and outright pissy. The good news is that you likely already have some practice dealing with someone you don't always agree with in your everyday life (Shannon in accounting, I'm looking at you), and you hopefully won't be inviting someone you absolutely loathe to travel with you anyway. No matter who you choose to travel with, prepare to both express yourself and actively listen. The trips I've taken with other people have been some of my absolute favorites and taking some time to think about your trip and the experience you want to have before asking someone to tag along can go a long way in making sure everyone has a good time.

Types of travel partners

Here's a general list of who you might be traveling with:

- Significant other
- Immediate family (spouse and kids)
- Other family (mom, dad, sister, brother, etc)
- Friends
- Big groups
- Coworkers

It's obvious but I'm going to say it anyway because it's important: your trip can take a very different tone depending on the type of relationship you have with your companion. The same restaurant, museum, or hike could all be vastly different experiences depending on who your companion is. Each type of companion can make each of those activities enjoyable in their own way, but just keep that the same person you love going to concerts with may or may not be the same person who is down for a 12 hour flight across the Pacific.

What to consider when choosing a travel companion

1. Make sure you have common interests. If you don't like a good chunk of similar activities, then it'll be a lot harder to compromise. If you hate museums and your partner wants to learn tons of facts about a place, it's not going to go well if you're hating being stuck in cold museums all day or if your partner has to miss out on learning about the place that interests them.

2. Agree on a budget beforehand. You've got to be on the same page here. Be clear on what you value spending money on and what amounts for certain activities will cause you distress. Create some ranges for big expenses, the rest can be filled in from there.

3. Don't bank on "opposites attract" going well. If someone's exceptionally talkative at all times of the day and you like to have long stretches alone with your thoughts, you might not be a good fit. If you're a "go with the flow" zen wanderer and your partner is a Type A plan-every-minute busy body, chances are it'll get pretty tense very quickly.

4. Matching personalities. You and whoever you choose to travel with should be able to have a good time in most situations. You don't have to be exactly the same, but if you have *very* different senses of humor, boundaries of acceptable dinner table conversations, willingness to debate politics, etc it might get a bit dicey.

5. Age matters. Family members might be a bit of an exception here, but it's worth keeping in mind regardless. The actual number of years between you may not be that important, but being in the same life stage does. A young 20 something who wants to go clubbing till morning may not be a great fit for a 30 something who wants to be in bed by 10 pm and up at 7 am.

6. Consider each other's strengths. We all have the things we're pretty good at, find out which of your strengths apply to traveling and use them to your advantage. This is a chance for your companion and you to really compliment each other when executed properly. If someone has a stronger sense of direction or memory for the path you've taken, maybe that person will take the lead on finding the way back if digital guidance fails. If someone is a better researcher, to find the best schedule for modes of transportation, maybe they take the lead there and call the shot.

#TravelTip: Try to take strong mental notes when leaving an Airbnb or hostel for about at least 5 minutes of walking or until you reach the major road. Notice a unique mural, or a certain shop's window display, anything to store in your memory when you're returning, either on foot or Uber's/Lyfts.

How to be a better travel companion:

It's so easy to get frustrated with others, but it can be very difficult to admit or acknowledge our own shortcomings. I think it's worth talking about how much of an impact our attitude can affect the well-being of ourselves as well as those around us. We can sour a moment or we can savor it. We can embrace chaos the best we can or we can be shut down by it. I'm not going to preach to you about how to be a good person, but just take the time to look at how your attitude and actions affect you and those around you. The first step you can take to having a great trip is deciding that you'll have fun no matter what gets thrown at you.

Recognize burnout or anxiety. While we tend to be more aware of our own emotions, it helps if we develop our skills to recognize others' emotions too. I can assure you that when your travel partner is feeling burnt out or anxious, doing things like yelling, scoffing, judging, etc is not going to make the situation better for either of you. Ask your partner what they're feeling and talk it through. Be patient and give them time to work through what they need to.

> "We have the tendency to want the other person to be a finished product while we give ourselves the grace to evolve."
> - T.D. Jakes.

With that being said, sometimes what your travel companion needs is a little tough love for motivation. I say a *little* very intentionally, there's a line between tough love and just being mean, so tread carefully.

With me and my travel partner in crime, there was a couple of times where they just needed to hear me put the truth out there when they were having a hard time continuing. When they were thinking we'd never make it to the boat we needed on time in Croatia, I told them I wasn't going to be satisfied unless we were literally running down the pier as it pulled away. Giving up 6 minutes away wasn't an option. When it came to finishing the uphill hike in the remote Porcupine Mountains, I told them there was only one way to get out and we could choose to finish in the daylight or the dark with rain coming. We laugh about those times now, so I'm assuming I wasn't too harsh, but sometimes you just have to put the reality of the situation out there to overcome some mental blocks. Slow and steady will take you very far, friends, don't give up.

Back to that spoonful of humility and empathy that I mentioned before, here are some tips on how to reflect on yourself as a travel companion.

- Always think before responding
- Make your intentions clear for what is important to you and what isn't
- Ask yourself, am I following the golden rule?
- Ask yourself, do I care enough to fight over this or can I let it go?
- Ask yourself, am I actually pulling my weight here or depending on them too much?
- Ask yourself, is there a snarky tone to my voice?
- Ask yourself, am I finding the positive in the situation or focusing on the negative?
- Get to know your triggers and communicate them early on
- Remember that your tone is extremely important
- If trying to have a "teaching moment", adapt to their learning style, not yours
- Take a personality test to get objective feedback. (I recommend 16personalities.com)

PERSONALITIES:

There's a lot of psychology behind what makes us who we are. I really enjoy the resources on 16personalities.com, they created a free test to get a "freakishly accurate" description of who you are and why you do things the way you do.

Their general breakdown is that our personalities are made up of 5 aspects and we fall somewhere on the spectrum of each between 2 types.

Five Personality Aspects		Sides of the Spectrum	
Mind	how we interact with our surroundings	Introvert	Extrovert
Energy	how we see the world and process information	Observant	Intuitive
Nature	how we make decisions and cope with emotions	Thinking	Feeling
Tactics	our approach to work, planning, and decision-making	Judging	Prospecting
Identity	how confident we are in our abilities and decisions	Assertive	Turbulent

There's no "better" personality or aspect. The key takeaway here is that we all fall in different places on these traits. It's important to be self-aware of where you fall and to be respectful and empathetic of how others handle situations differently than we do. The better we are at being aware and empathetic, the quicker, easier, and more effectively we can resolve conflicts and get to have a great time!

There's a delicate balance between getting what you want out of the trip and accomplishing the same for who you're with. If you think about it as a scale (Shout out to all my Libras), the scales are constantly in motion, slightly teetering back and forth but should remain relatively level. Hopefully by the time you're on the plane you and your companion or group have already hashed out the major wants and game plan. It's okay if you need to go your separate ways sometimes!

A little breather from being with someone 24/7 can be a good thing. So if you need time apart, just nicely tell who you're with that you are just used to having a bit of alone time. And if someone is letting you know they need some space, respect their wishes.

CONFLICT MANAGEMENT

Let's say some tension has been building for a few days about the best way to use your last day in the country you're in. Your original plan got squashed when you found out the main attraction you wanted to see is under construction and not open the day you were planning to see it. You and your friend are trying not to step on each other's toes as you throw out new ideas.

1. **Be clear** on what you would like, and why. Be clear on what your alternatives are.
2. **Don't be defensive.** Accept the past for what it is and work towards a solution, not towards justifying your ego. Placing blame doesn't help move forward either.
3. **Prioritize resolving the conflict over being right.** It's better in the long run.
4. **Actively listen.** Maybe the root issue is just a matter of truly hearing them out.
5. **Keep calm.** Nothing gets better when we raise our voices or use a sour tone.
6. **Don't take things personally.** The world doesn't revolve around you and their reasoning probably doesn't either.
7. **Be quick to apologize and forgive.** If all it takes to improve the situation is saying "I'm sorry", is that worth it?
8. **Try Top 3.** One of you suggests your top 3 choices and the other pick their favorite of the 3.

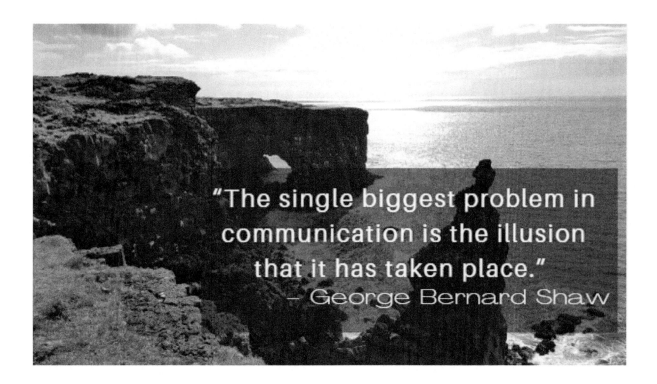

"The single biggest problem in communication is the illusion that it has taken place."
– George Bernard Shaw

Don't go with Debbie Downer

Let me pop more bubbles. There's a chance that the person who wants to travel with you might not be a good fit for you or the type of trip you're looking to have. That's okay! Tactfully tell them. Strongly consider honesty first, but say what you have to. I'm here to encourage you to have the trip of your dreams and I'll be the first to say that who you travel with can have a huuuuge impact on that for better or for worse.

Don't go with Debbie Downer or the friend who can never compromise on where to go out on a Friday night let alone on the decisions you have to make abroad. Don't go with the family member who always finds a way to talk 90% of the time about themselves. Don't go with someone who wants to sit in the room because it's sprinkling when you can still make the best out of the day. If you need permission from someone to get you to follow your gut, then this is me giving it to you. If you need someone else to be the bad guy here, email me and I'll break the bad news to them myself. You only have control over your own attitude, not everyone else's, so don't waste precious time on people who you know in your heart will only take and not give.

So what should you do if you're now realizing the travel partner you had in mind might not actually be the best fit for you? Consider solo traveling. It's terrifying but incredibly rewarding.

SOLO TRAVEL

There's a reason why there are so many blogs about traveling alone. It's amazing! Terrifying, but amazing. Personally, I grew up with very strong feelings of fear surrounding the idea of being alone and have struggled with them into my adult life. I can honestly say that pushing myself to travel alone has been single-handedly the greatest step I've taken to coping and resolving those fears. I feel indescribably stronger, more capable, confident, and assured in ways that I can feel in all parts of my life, like work and personal relationships. Maybe you don't have those same fears or insecurities that I did, I sure hope not. But everyone can benefit from solo travel in their own ways.

Do you feel like you're meant for more than what's around you in your little town?
Do you have a hard time making decisive decisions in the moment?
Do you struggle with time management?
Do you feel like you lack self-control or will power?
Do you feel overwhelmed with duties and responsibilities to others?
Do you feel like you get pushed around by those in your life?
Do you feel an urge to be connected to something bigger than yourself?
Do you feel like you've never taken a risk and have been playing things too safe?

It's okay to want more for ourselves while being grateful for what we have; they're not mutually exclusive. If you answered yes to any of those questions, I'm willing to bet that solo travel would be a great means of personal growth for you. How? It's simple. When you travel alone, you have to make all the decisions, plan things out, and make them happen. Sounds like a lot of work, but think about it: You get to do all the activities YOU want to do. Eat wherever sounds great to you. You don't have to consider anyone else's opinions and get the opportunity to start listening to the beat of your drum. You can go on the trip when you make the time for it, not have to coordinate with someone else's timeline. You can get up when you want and spend as much or as little time wandering as you want.

I know I said that the memories you make with your favorite people are more valuable than the trip itself, but sometimes that person is you. Humans are social creatures, we find strength in numbers and are typically better when we put our heads together. But in today's world, we're overwhelmed by input from thousands of people every day. We're overstimulated by expectations from having access to the news, social media, our social network. How are we supposed to decipher between what we actually want vs what society tells us to want unless we take the time to sort through it all? Solo travel is an incredible way to be with your thoughts, put distance between you and your "normal life" to view things from a different perspective, to shun the constant feedback that you should be a certain way. It gives us the opportunity to push ourselves towards paths that we might not have gone down otherwise.

So when it comes to solo travel, here's my call to action for you.

CALL TO ACTION

- REJECT THE NOTION THAT YOU NEED SOMEONE WITH YOU TO TRAVEL.

- REJECT THAT BEING ALONE AUTOMATICALLY MEANS BEING SAD AND LONELY.

- REJECT THAT YOU'RE NOT SMART, BRAVE, OR CAPABLE ENOUGH, OF TRAVELING ON YOUR OWN.

- BELIEVE THAT YOU'RE FULLY WILLING AND ABLE TO MAKE YOUR DREAM TRIP COME TO FRUITION WHETHER YOU HAVE SOMEONE TO GO WITH OR NOT.

Solo Trip in Portugal 2018 (Sintra, Portugal at Pena Palace)

GROUP TRIPS

Ahhh, group trips. I love that big life events can result in group trips like bachelor(ette) getaways. I love the idea of annual trips to reconnect with friends. I love the idea of spur of the moment "let's all go to Mardis Gras!" trips. I love that you get to split the cost with more people making additional options affordable.

There's a ton to love about traveling with groups of friends, family, or tours. That super expensive, gorgeous Airbnb house that is $300 a night with a hot tub and a minimum of 3 night stay? That'll take a chunk out of anyone's travel budget, but split it with 6 of your buddies and now you've got a great weekend that's less likely to break the bank.

However, traveling with more people comes with more scheduling conflicts, surplus of opinions, and more compromises to be made. Keeping open minds, communicating openly, and practicing patience are key to smooth, less stressful trips.

My advice for those who are taking the lead on planning or coordinating:
- Start the conversation early
- Be clear on deadlines to commit and what you're offering/asking
- Ask for clarity frequently so you're on the same page
- Make planning as visual as possible, the more people there are to coordinate with the more there is to keep track of.

Create a document or chat that you can share with the group, start a facebook event, take a poll, etc. Do what you need to do to make it easier on everyone to understand, resulting in less stress for you.

My advice for those who are participating:
- Give more details than less, think about what you'd want to know if you were planning this and include that in your responses
  - If someone asks more than one question, answer both clearly
  - If you don't know, then just say you don't know yet. That's much more helpful than silence.
- Be willing to compromise
- Offer to help, the planner has their normal life and responsibilities too. Share the burden.
- Respect others responses
- Look at any resources provided to you for answers *before* asking questions
- Don't be a mooch, pay your own way. It's not on others to provide for you.

Feel free to use my travel planner Collectingthepostcards.com.

Seattle, Washington USA

BONUS

Need something to pass the time or lighten the mood?

I have a pretty cool ability to make a game out of just about anything when I'm bored. Here are some of my favorites while traveling.

Hairdos.
Look around the crowd and try to find two people with the same hairdo. When I play, color doesn't matter, just the cut and length. You can be as picky or easygoing as you want to be.

Dog names.
When you see puppers, guess what their name might be, or what you'd want it to be.

Fake life.
This one's a little harder and requires more imagination, but it can be fun while your creativity is flowing. Look at someone, and come up with their back story or their life details. It's pretty much like what Jake and Charles do on Brooklyn Nine Nine. #terrylovesyogurt

Relationships

When you see two people walking together, guess what their relationship is with each other. Some are pretty easy but some are total wildcards. It's fun in restaurants when you get more of a chance to sneak glances every once in a while instead of them just walking by.

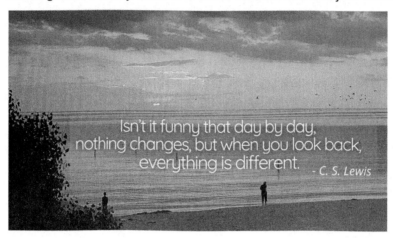

Isn't it funny that day by day, nothing changes, but when you look back, everything is different. - C. S. Lewis

The important takeaway here is that you're spending this time with the *right* person at that point in time. One of the biggest life lessons that I've learned through traveling is that sharing those memories with your favorite people is a thousand times more valuable than the destination.

As we look back on our most valuable memories, the ones that are spent with the people we cherish the most. And maybe you haven't found that person yet, maybe you'll meet them while on your next adventure. I believe everything happens when it's supposed to happen, maybe a trip with your best friend is just what you need right now. Maybe a getaway weekend with your mom is what your soul is longing for. Do some self-reflection and the answers should become clearer.

KEY TAKEAWAYS OF THE WHO

- Self reflection, active listening, and compromise are invaluable tools in travel and in life
- You may love someone but not want to travel with them, and that's okay. Choose wisely depending on the trip type.
- Don't go with Debbie downer, it's not worth it.
- Solo Travel can be incredible and an opportunity to learn a ton about yourself.
- Take a step back and make sure you're being the best travel companion you can be before pointing fingers.
- Conflict Management is better sooner than later.
- Always try to look at the bright side and find the fun in travel, joy is contagious.

3	**THE WHO** Companions	• Decide on traveling companions (if not yet determined) • Talk with companions about their wants, don't wants and expectations • Find common interests and split up planning duties

THE WHERE

Go where the most activities you like are. Not because of a picture.

Look at you go, pal! You're killing it!

You've thought about *WHY* it's important to you to make this trip happen, you've pondered *WHAT* you'd like to do, and *WHO* you want to go with (*or without*)!

Now let's figure out *WHERE* is the best place to do it.

Take everything that you and your travel buddies put on your wish list of activities and start looking at the best destinations to do those things. Hopefully, you agreed on most things, but use this chance to bring compromises to the table!

I'm not here to suggest my favorite spots or push you towards where I've been because this book is about how to make YOUR dream trip happen. **You just have to read through the advice in the How section and do your research for what suits you and your travel party the best.**

PICTURES VS REALITY

I have to be a bummer here and let you in on a secret. Some places look great in pictures, but just aren't worth taking the time to visit. Some pictures have such a mood that pulls you in, however, there just might not be enough to do there to make your time and money worth the visit.

For example, I'm obsessed with the cherry blossoms blooming in Japan. I feel like my heart would explode with happiness if I got to wander around among the trees in all their pinkish white glory. However, I know that I recently went to Japan (during non cherry blossom season, sad) and that I have other places with more to offer me than just pretty petals on trees.

It's important to distinguish what picture we enjoy looking at vs what places we'd actually get maximum value out of. Another example I see a lot is pretty breakfast spots in Italy overlooking the Mediterarean. Gorgeous pictures, right?! That Amalfi Coast looks amazing in pictures on those bright beautiful days. I fully intend to see it in person because I know that the Amalfi Coast offers activities and tours I want to spend my time, money and energy on, not solely because of the pretty breakfast picture. You with my logic here? Take a minute to think about what your day would look like before and after that picture. Look some ideas up, then decide if you'd like to put in on your list of serious contenders.

UNDERGROUND VS SUPER POPULAR

FOR CITIES:
Depending on your interests, some places will be worth the hype and sometimes the underground place will be more than you could have imagined. There's no way of knowing for sure until you vett them for yourself!

I'm not going to tell you to skip a certain place because it might actually be great for you! (except Leaning Tower of Pisa, never heard of anyone having fun there) Honestly, my room was decorated in a Paris theme for all of high school and it's actually really low on my favorites list. Everyone is different. You might fall head over heels in love with Paris and all it has to offer!

In my personal experience, for super popular places in cities sometimes the fun is the energy from everyone there and sometimes it's so draining to deal with all the people. Sometimes the underground spot is spectacular and has such a vibe and other times it's so boring and feels like wasted time. There is no magic formula or way to know which will be which, the best you can do is weed out the places that don't fit your fancy and be willing to roll with the punches.

I will recommend that you at least seek out the underground, less popular options when you can before just defaulting to the popular destinations. But either way, it'll all be fine as long as you stay positive and find the good parts in everything. Choose to make the best of it and you'll have a good time no matter what.

Busiest Crosswalk in the World. Tokyo, Japan

FOR NATURE:

Again, just my personal experience, but I'm going to flip flop the opinion of cities above. When it comes to nature, it's soooooo much better to have the place to yourself. It's way more fun (to me, at least) to explore off the beaten path and find the hidden gems. Then I can dance around, skip like a kid, make tons of loud bad jokes, climb on stuff I'm probably not supposed to, and be a total dork.

Nature has a ton to offer, a sense of peace being my favorite. And nothing ruins that like a family with yelling kids (sorry families, do what you have to do!) and getting stuck behind a slow group on a trail. Some of the super popular places are pretty cool for a reason. Sure, they have some cool features or views, but the people around are usually so distracting that it's hard to get the full impact of that coolness.

It's sometimes harder to go in the off season because of extreme weather, but you'd be amazed at the places you can find where no one else is. Seek and ye shall find, my baby birds, seek and ye shall find.

"Just when you think it can't get any worse, it can. And just when you think it can't get any better, it can."
— Nicholas Sparks

RECOMMENDATION!

Back on cities again, I have a recommendation for you to look at while you're researching.
Sandemans NEW EUROPE walking tours and other experiences.

I LOVE THIS COMPANY. They have cities mostly across Europe that have locals provide walking tours multiple times a day for free to show you their beautiful cities. All you have to do is sign up and tip your tour guide whatever you feel they deserved. (Tip them well because they're almost always spectacular!) Look for the red umbrellas in the meeting spots they describe online.

I've gone on probably 7 of these tours now and I loved every single one, especially when I'm traveling alone. I even made 2 friends on one of these tours in Lisbon who I got to hang out with for the next 2 days. Changed my entire time in that city.

I usually sign up for the time slots that I'm arriving in so they can help me get my bearings of the city. They have awesome commentary, sometimes in multiple languages. There are typically English, Spanish, and Chinese tours.

They have other experiences available on their website too for reasonable prices that highlight some of the amazing culture in that city. I've done 3 or 4 of those experiences and they've been amazing. These tour guides are sometimes the same as the walking tours, so if you really love a guide, you can ask if they're hosting any other experiences. They'll probably promote it themselves, though. Be sure to leave them awesome reviews if you enjoyed it, your support goes a long way.

15/10 would recommend. #NotaSponsor

TAKE ADVANTAGE OF THE UNEXPECTED

I've had a lot of great experiences in places that were never on my radar, that I would never have known to research or look into. Despite being the super planner that I am, even I know that you can't plan everything. There's such joy to the spontaneous adventures that pop up. Go after those moments whenever you can. Again, focus on the positive and sometimes the unexpected road bump turns into a great time and even greater story.

Example: Being only a few feet away from being squashed

to death by a MASSIVE tree from an unexpected wind storm in Oregon (which also trapped us in the campground with no way to get our van out) while a forest fire was out of control one town over and it was raining ash from an apocalyptic orange smokey sky? Scary as hell.

But now it's a day I'm really proud of myself for handling it. Did I feel sick from panic? Absolutely. But now I'm stronger because I can look back at things less life threatening and know that it'll be okay.

Culture

I cannot begin to express how interesting culture is to me. Part of a destination's beauty comes from it's people, their culture, and history. When deciding where the best place for you to spend time, I urge you to not leave out that important cultural piece. It'll be a huge part of your experience there and can add more richness to your memories than you could ever anticipate, whether you're there for a day or a month.

But what is culture, you may ask?

Culture is defined as **the customs, arts, social institutions, and achievements of a particular nation, people, or other social group.** It's the fabric that weaves groups of people in close proximity together. It's a beautiful representation of their way of living.

Culture is a lot of things. It's holidays, festivals, language, fashion, hobbies, architecture, music, traditions.

To me, culture is the passage of customs down generations as the terrain shapes the people, and in turn the attitudes and beliefs of the people shape the modern day world that we see today.

It's the reason why you'll see cows wandering and grazing in India because they view cows as "a sacred symbol of life that should be protected and revered".

It's why Mexico celebrates Dia de los Muertos as a practice from their Aztec ancestry to honor their dead around All Saints Day or All Souls Day.

It's why you'll hear a lot of slurping in Japanese restaurants as a sort of compliment to the chef.

Pictured: Udon Noodles in Kyoto, Japan

There are endless examples of culture because we're lucky to have such amazing diversity. No matter where you're from, you grew up surrounded by your regional culture whether you realise it or not. For my fellow Americans, have you ever thought about why we say "Bless you" after someone sneezes? There probably wasn't a moment where someone taught you to do that, you probably just picked it up over time when you were young.

Side Note: These are the best noodles I've had in my life. We went back the next day, which is basically a no-no in my travel style, but they were too amazing not to have again.

Potty time
Let's talk about the bathrooms, shall we? European Bathrooms specifically.

There's some situations you should be aware of so they don't totally catch you off guard. First of all, across Europe they're usually called toilettes or WC (Water closet) which in French, is pronounced sort of like doob-la-say. In England it might be called the Loo in conversation but I saw more WC signs than anything.

It's fairly common to have to pay a small fee to use public restrooms in large cities or transportation ports whether that be to an attendant outside the bathroom or a coin machine to gain entry. It's usually between 15 cents-1 euro, probably in the 50 cent range most often. The general idea is that the fee goes towards paying someone to clean the bathroom and buy the toilet paper, etc.

While we Americans may be a bit off put by this, it's just another thing to get used to. There are plenty of other options in establishments but with the expectation that you buy something in exchange, like a coffee at a cafe.

Now, I will say I've seen some sketchy looking "attendants" that I'm pretty sure were just panhandlers. It's up to you how you want to handle it if you suspect the same thing, you can try to walk by and refuse them, you can just pay it, you can turn around and look for a different bathroom.

There are also sometimes port-a-potties look-alikes that are a bit more structural that you may find on the streets, usually with a WC sign. They might need coins to open the door, might not. Just like anywhere, you never know what state the inside will be or the last time it was cleaned, but it's an option when you're desperate.

All I can say is good luck, keep some loose change when you're in major cities, and use the bathrooms when you see the nice ones.

Learning cultural norms and history

While you don't have to spend a ton of time getting to know the country or city's entire history, it's important to learn the cultural norms of the area. Examples: if they're conservatively dressed, the reason for a certain holiday, actions you can't do there, how to show respect or avoid being disrespectful, etc.

Take 15-20 minutes to look at dos and don'ts of that country and a summary of their history. Chances are someone's already done the hard work for you and posted an article on it for whatever country or city you're looking for.

Some examples of important cultural norms:
Gifts are extremely valued in most Asian countries. so much so that in Japan, business people will receive your business card with both hands, handle it delicately, and put it in their jacket pocket because it's considered rude to put it in your back pocket (near the heart is more respectful than near the butt). It's also taboo to give things in sets of four because the number four is pronounced the same as death.

In China, one should never give someone an umbrella as it suggests that you want this friendship to end or separate in Chinese Culture.

In Europe, la bise (French term for a series of light kisses on the cheeks) is a normal greeting for friends and family but different areas have their own number of kisses to give. Some areas might only do one on both cheek, other areas might do left, right, left, and other areas might do two kisses on each cheek. Someone might say hello or goodbye in this manner once they're comfortable with you, and it can take you off guard if you aren't aware of the custom.

In Saudi Arabia, you should always eat with your right hand, your left is considered unsanitary (the wiping hand). You should always bring a gift if you're invited to someone's house, which is common. It's also very common for men to walk holding hands and the standard of "personal space" is much closer than individuals from the US might be used to. It's also taboo to show someone the bottom of your shoes and to point at people.

In a lot of countries, you need to request the bill when you're finished, they will not bring it to you as it's custom to enjoy long lunches and stay for hours.

Each country has its own cultural norms, so be sure to do your due diligence to be prepared and respectful to the locals. There's a lot of tools on Pinterest and Google that summarize the key points to know for travelers.

Somewhere in Southeast Asia

Culture Shock

Now all of this might feel overwhelming, I understand. That brings me to my next point, culture shock.

Culture shock is the feeling of disorientation experienced by someone who is suddenly subjected to an unfamiliar culture, way of life, or set of attitudes.

It can be so overwhelming and chaotic when you show up someplace and everything is incredibly different than what you're used to. It takes time to adjust, get our bearings, and process what's going on around us when we show up somewhere new. Typically it applies to people who move or stay for extended periods of time, but I think it's fair to say that there's a mini version for when you first show up anywhere drastically different than your usual.

You're probably familiar with the general concept so we can leave it at that, so instead let's focus on what you can do when you feel that jolt of culture shock.

If you show up excited by the new sights, sounds, and smells, Awesome! Enjoy that excitement! On the other hand, if you're feeling a little stressed or stretched too thin at that moment, my advice is very similar to anyone feeling overwhelmed or feeling the start of a panic attack.

My process is this:
1. Identify that I'm feeling overwhelmed
2. Take 5 deep breaths
3. Try to get somewhere that's a bit calmer
4. Remember that this is only temporary
5. Tell myself it's all okay, it just takes time to adjust

Everything will be okay! If you're with someone who seems to be having a harder time adjusting, just remember to be empathetic and have a little patience. We all process things differently and at our own pace.

Key Takeaways of The Where:

- Some places are better experienced as social media pictures than trip destinations
- Cities' super popular spots might/might not be worth it. That's for you to decide.
- Nature is almost always better off the beaten path.
- Take advantage of the unexpected! Follow the spontaneous moments.
- Places all around the world have their own culture, it'll shape your experience
- Take the time to research a bit on cultural norms before you go (Dos and Don'ts)
- Culture Shock is real but everything will be okay! Give yourself time to adjust.

4 THE WHERE Destinations

- Research the best locations to do the activities you and your travel companion(s) are interested in
- Decide where you're going!
- Begin looking at logistics of getting there (preliminary planning)

Phi Phi Island, Thailand

If you never go, you'll never know.

THE WHEN

The best time is off season, but anytime is better than never.

The When

Why wait for a new year when a new day is already here.
- Unknown

Let me start with the biggest, most valuable, important, impactful point:

Now is the time to make this happen.

It may not be the day that you leave on the trip itself, but today can be the day that you promise yourself you're going to see this through to completion.

Today can be the day you get started.
Today can be the day that you take that next big step.
Today can be the day you book an important piece of the trip.
Today can be the day you get the framework figured out.

DO NOT WAIT FOREVER, because forever isn't waiting for you. Time will fly by whether you like it or not. Carve out time **now** in the near future to make this dream come true for yourself.

I know, I know, life happens and there's a lot of variables. But we have control over more than we usually think we do, we just need to be brave enough to ask or make it happen. Life will go on with us out of town for a few days. I also know it takes time to be in a financial position to make trips happen, so again, START NOW for your future self.

Okay, point made. Moving on.

Let's pretend that you have all sorts of free time and you have to decide when is the best time to go based on your destination instead of a timeline dictated by life.

Factors to consider when researching when to travel

Some seasons might better than others because of the following:

Weather changes-

The shoulder seasons (usually spring and fall) are sometimes cheaper because there's a higher chance of less than ideal weather. It may be cooler during the day or nights, might be more likely to rain or be cloudy, might be hurricane season or the time of year where seaweed washes up everywhere, etc. There are lots of weather-related effects on price depending on where you go.

Exceptions to the spring and fall might be summer in super hot places or winter in arctic places. Like Las Vegas, for example, it's basically torture to do anything outside in daylight hours in the middle of summer in that desert heat and sun, so winter, fall, and spring would be more of the peak seasons.

Keep in mind though, that the seasons might be drastically different in the months that you're used to them being in. For me in the Midwest, USA, I'm blessed and cursed with all four seasons that I personally break down like this:

SPRING = late March-May
SUMMER = June-early September
AUTUMN (Fall) = Late September-November
WINTER = December- early March

But in Northern Europe, it's different. In Australia, or anywhere in the southern hemisphere, it's polar opposites! So keep that in mind when booking. Months do not equal the weather you're used to.

Tip: always do a quick internet search of the weather and the month you're thinking of visiting. Ex) *"São Paulo, Brazil weather in March"* *(It's the transition from summer to winter)*

Less crowds

Probably because of the weather, some seasons are better to visit because there will be fewer crowds. Old City in Dubrovnik, Croatia is encased in 13th Century walls that do not leave a lot of pushing room in the 3 feet wide side alleys. So, Spring and Fall offer a much less cramped experience if you're able to catch some nice weather without being shoved and caught in the crowds.

Other people are busy

Let's face it, waiting in long lines or not being able to do an activity because it's already booked or full is not fun. Maybe you can give yourself an edge by looking at going during a non-prime time season.

I have a lot of friends that say Disney World in October is the best time because it's still warm, has a Halloween theme, but there are fewer crowds because the school group hype has passed! In the US, most schools are on summer break between June and September, so that's the time when a ton of families take their vacations. Great!...except that means more lines, more kids, more waiting, and more money down the drain.

If you're able to travel during different months to places that families might flock to, then awesome! Do it whenever you can, but even if you can't, look into some ways to avoid the crowds online. People share tips and tricks about shortcuts and ways to beat the crowds at popular locations all the time. Some research might get you way ahead of the others.

Story Time:
At the Anne Frank House in Amsterdam, Netherlands, my bestie and I were able to skip a line THREE BLOCKS long just because we booked a time slot online instead of just showing up. The looks we got as we waltzed right past the hordes of tourists to walk right in with no wait was hilarious, to say the least. The time slots were only about 20 minutes long since it's not a large space at all and everyone has to keep moving in, through, and back out fairly quickly. Still, being able to skip that wait gives me a cool memory of the Anne Frank House instead of the memory of waiting to get into the house.

#TravelTip: I'd recommend that if you find yourself waiting in a long line, do some quick online searching to see if there's a way to skip it. Doesn't hurt to try! Something to do in the meantime.

Deeper dive into activities

Remember those dream activities we thought so much about in the What? We definitely want to make sure what you want to do is available at the time you're going to be on your trip!

Okay, you've got a pretty good sense of what you want to do while you're traveling, got your eye on certain tours or activities. If you haven't already researched if those book up quickly, do it now. Some activities need to be booked weeks or months in advance, find out if what you're interested in doing is one of those things. Once that is done, you still need to take a deeper dive into the activities that don't need to be booked way in advance, but still might need to know a few things ahead of time to make your life easier.

At some point, you need to look at the details of the activities you want to do like the days they're open and hours of operation so you can plan them accordingly. Or at least know when they are available if you're going more with the flow.

Let's say you want to visit a museum or botanic gardens. Great! You plan on going only to show up and they're not even open. What?! How could they not be open?! Well, some museums or other activities are open to the public on weekends, so they close on a weekday to do the maintenance or upkeep that's necessary. Be sure to not make assumptions when planning on going somewhere. Maybe it's a national holiday that you're not familiar with and didn't plan around everything being closed that day. Google, call, send the email, do what you have to do ahead of time to have a better idea how you can plan your general timeline of activities.

Some tours and excursions only run on certain days of the week, especially during the shoulder seasons (usually that country's spring and fall). Some activities might not be available at all during the off seasons. Think snorkeling trips in December when you're not near the equator. Be prepared and do your research, it'll only take a few minutes to do, but could derail your whole plan or expectations if you don't. It's the same concept with checking the hours, it's better to find out for sure about the activities you really want to make happen.

You won't find the time. You have to make the time. I wish we all had lives that we could go explore whenever we feel like it, but most of us can't just pack up and leave to travel everytime we feel like it. But we CAN plan for it and take steps to making it a priority, taking the time off, and not giving up on it when it may get messy.

How long
There's no perfect length of a trip, there are too many factors that differ for each of us.

Just use the time that you carved out to the best of your ability to fill it with as many amazing memories that you can!

5 THE WHEN Timelines

- Research destination for ideal times to go and weather conditions for your preferred time of travel
- Establish a window of opportunity to travel with your companion(s)
- Begin hammering our details of when you're going!

"Exchange what you've always known for what you've always wanted."

Urquhart Castle on Loch Ness, Scotland

THE HOW

Time to nail down the details, welcome to the exciting part!

PLANNING

THE TIME HAS FINALLY COME. Planning. Whether the idea of planning gets you pumped or makes you cringe, it's the next step to making those amazing memories. I can't stress enough how important planning is but it doesn't have to be a terrible experience. As I've preached endlessly, the planning you do now will allow you to more thoroughly enjoy the experience later. Road bumps are inevitable but you can minimize them by preparing now. This stage is going to be a whirlwind of moving pieces as you explore your options, so embrace the chaos. It'll be so incredibly worth it in the end. This is where your caterpillar ideas get to become beautiful butterflies.

6 — **THE HOW** Details

- Begin putting a tentative plan together with companion(s)
- Book activities, accommodations, transportation, and making preparations for trip
- Finalize details and get ready for your dream trip!

*"He who has a **why** to live can bear almost any **how**."*

— Friedrich Nietzsche

REMINDER!

I MADE A WORKBOOK FOR YOU!

Collectingthepostcards.com for the Google Sheets, Excel or PDF versions.

Use this workbook to help you fill in the details of your trip!

How to break it down

If you're anything like me, get ready to have 10+ tabs open at all times as you explore the interwebs for all the deals and details. Your search is going to get overwhelming at one point or another or another but it's only temporary. Walk away when you need to, go destress for a while and come back when you're ready (Just don't give up!). We all have our different processes, so do what's best for you. Here's what works for me, tweak it to work for you.

I'm a list maker. I even wrote this book by breaking it down to a list of key points I wanted to talk about. Whether it's on paper, notes on your phone, or a word doc, write down somewhere what you need to do. It can be as high-level or as detailed as you want, just get it down somewhere. Writing this down helps in a few ways by giving it a place to live outside of your head, gives it merit as something you actually plan on doing, and gives you a place to mark progress and get your next topic to look into.

There are a few ways you can set it up:
- by location (city or country) if you're making multiple stops
- by timeline (especially helps if you have a general idea of how many days you'll spend where)
- by category, Ex) all transportation together, activities, accommodations, etc.
- To do and completed (make a list of everything to do, move it to the done side when finished)

Whatever works for you is what's best. You might start one way and completely change it by the time you're done. You might make this list and barely touch it as you still make progress on planning. That's all okay! The important part is, and will always be, that you actually go on the trip of your dreams and you have an awesome time. Planning is just a step in making that a reality, so don't stress too much, alright?

Focus on the fun! Is there something you're super excited to look into? Go for it! I find it works for me to start with the fun because it sucks me in and then I can fall into a groove where I get a bunch done. Finding that calling (activity, attraction, etc) makes it easier to get started. Throw in a few not-so-fun details like train schedules once you're on a roll.

Key Largo, Florida

Keeping track of everything

I'm a huge fan of either keeping a ton of tabs open or copying the link onto my sheet and then typing a little summary so I can know what the link is to when I look at it later. It's super helpful to also stick to a standard in your document/list. Standards help keep things from looking totally chaotic, so if you paste a link and put your summary on the line underneath it, continue to do that for all other links. If you switch it up and type above it or on the same line, it might get confusing what summary belongs to what link. It's also easy to get muddled from having tons of font colors, inconsistent bold, underlining, etc. Just keep it simple.

Ex) https://www.delta.com/us/en/baggage/carry-on-baggage
Delta Airline: one personal item and one carry on included with the flight

Use the same email when booking things and consider creating a standard travel-related login to have the same password. I know, I know, you shouldn't use the same password for everything. But it's a nightmare to try to remember the password for the login you bought train tickets on 6 months ago when you're trying to just log in to see your confirmation details. Don't even get me started on how tough it is when your laptop has all your auto logins saved and you're trying to do it on your phone. Choose a password for the one-time-use travel logins that you'll inevitably create along with the planning phase. Make sure it's different from any bank, school, emails, and other personal logins that you have, but it'll make it easy when you're abroad or away and need to get in quickly. I have a travel password that I change about every year or so but it makes it easy for all things related to that trip.

I usually take pictures or screenshots of my confirmation details, dates, times, etc., and keep it in a certain folder on my phone so I can get to it extremely easily. It saves time, battery life, data, and my sanity when I'm feeling super anxious about mixing up dates or times. Having the details at your fingertips helps when you're there in person and need to plan out when you need to leave by or reference them quickly.

Key Takeaways for Initial Planning:

- Make a list of what you need to do
- Save links in one document for easy reference with summaries
- Use the same email for confirmations, tickets, details, etc
- Take pictures or screenshots of relevant details (QR codes, barcodes with dates, times, company names, etc)

Planning with your traveling companion

Thank goodness for the internet, amiright? It's so much easier to share information than ever before, so use it to share your research with your travel companion. Set up some sort of home base on a Google sheet or doc (or anything similar) for your research and what you end up deciding on. It's awesome to be able to see what each other has done, have a timeline of recent changes, and be able to comment on stuff without changing it.

You're going to have to:
- split up responsibilities
- set up a timeline
- compromise
- triage what each of you cares most about
- communicate what types of details you can decide for the both of you and what you'll need to get approval before confirming
- tactfully hold each other accountable
- keep track of what's done and left to do

FLIGHTS

We're going to cover a bunch of topics regarding flying like how it all works, booking flights, general tips, and things to consider. We're going to go veeeerrryy in depth here because I think that flying might be the scariest part for a lot of people. I want to take some of that uncertainty out of the equation so you can have a better idea of what to expect.

First of all, I hope to put those who are afraid of flying at ease. Flying opens up the world to you! It can get you across the state, country, or globe in a matter of hours. It seems scary to be in a machine that can fly but it's incredibly safe, painless, and convenient. Don't let an irrational fear keep you from amazing experiences, foods, and memories. There's nothing like getting to be above the clouds and see the world from a different perspective.

If you're not familiar with airport lingo, it can be overwhelming and confusing, so if you find it useful, check out this list of vocab. If you feel comfortable with the lingo, just skip ahead to the next part. No hard feelings.

Some general flight vocabulary in my own words:

Book a flight - Buy a ticket or a seat on a plane
TSA - Transportation Security Administration (TSA)
Carry on - the bag that you get to "carry on" with you onto the plane. Typically the small suitcase or backpack size. The luggage goes up in the bins above the seats or under your seat in front of you. Each airline can make their own size limit.
Personal Item - Small bag, purse, camera bag, or laptop case. Usually goes under the seat, where you should keep the items that you want access to during the flight.
Checked bag - The luggage that's larger, typically a suitcase with wheels. You "check" your luggage into the airline providers at booths typically right by where you enter the airport. The airline tags it and delivers it to the plane and when you get off at your destination, they send it to the Baggage Claim carousel for you to pick up.
Baggage Claim - A rotating conveyor belt where they unload luggage from the plane for passengers to pick up. They have screens that say what flight's luggage is on what carousel.
Gates - It's the "gateway" from the airport to the airplane. It's essentially a waiting area with an airline rep at a door that you walk through to board the plane. Each plane gets assigned a gate to take off from and to come to when they land so everyone knows where to go (passengers, airline staff, luggage, airport staff).

Terminal - It's basically a building where all the gates are located that planes can taxi up to. The bigger the airport, the more terminals. Some airports call them by names (Detroit has McNamara and North Terminals) and others go by letters or numbers (Terminal A, B, C, or Terminal 1, 2, 3, etc). It's very possible that you'll need to take a train, bus, or shuttle to get from one terminal to the other. For connection flights, most airlines stay in one terminal so there's not often a need to switch.

Concourse - is a subarea within a terminal that helps distinguish which direction you should go as airport terminals typically have "wings". They're usually named by letters (concourse A, B, C). I think they're mostly helpful to just direct you towards the right part of the building, just follow the signs above you in the airport.

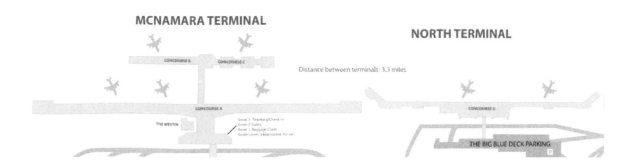

LOOKING AT FLIGHTS

Flights are often the biggest single expense that you'll have on a trip (if you're flying of course). Unless you're going to choose where you go based on the cheapest flight you can get, chances are that you're going to have to pay whatever is available when you sit down to book. Luckily, some smart planning and tricks can increase your odds of finding better prices on flights.

Let's look at different factors that affect plane ticket prices. Skipping the economics behind how and why airlines do certain things and set the prices they do (although it is super fascinating!...to me); I'm just going to summarize the factors that are most likely to affect you as a passenger and the price you'll pay.

Direct vs. connection - Direct flights are so much more convenient and faster, but that often comes with a higher price tag. Connection flights are usually cheaper because of the inconvenience but they open up so many more flight options. If you had to wait for direct flights to everywhere you wanted to go, you'd be stuck for a while.

Time of year - Everywhere has busy and slow seasons, usually because of weather, so keep that in mind when planning your trip. The busy season will cost you more and have more packed flights. Try to find the sweet spots between the seasons. Keep in mind that the hemispheres have "opposite" seasons, so Australian winter is not the same time as in the USA

Holidays - Beyond just season, flying around or on actual holidays can have a HUGE effect on the prices, often insanely higher, but every once in a while there are some last-minute deals. Keep in mind other countries have different holidays than we do.

Length - How far you're traveling obviously has an impact, but it's not as much as you might expect. It might cost you $200 to get a flight somewhere in the same state and also halfway across the country.

Destination - If you're going somewhere with a huge airport, then you'll have more options to choose from. Like CDG in Paris or ATL in Atlanta, for example. But if you're trying to go somewhere more remote, that usually comes with an added cost. Getting to the Maldives for example, would likely be more expensive flights because there is less demand, infrastructure and flight options. Supply and demand control the price and it's harder to supply a flight to a small island chain in the Indian Ocean.

How long in advance you book - This one has a HUGE impact on the price you pay. There's no clear-cut answer on the exact amount of days you should book in advance or the day of the week for the best deals. There probably never will be. A general rule is typically 30-90 days before your flight.

Airline Hubs - Each airline has their hubs which are kind of like "home" airports that they have a lot of gates and flights from there. Flights are usually a bit cheaper to and from hubs because they make those flights often. You can usually get a sense of what the hubs are by looking at the connection fight locations. If multiple flights have connections to the same airport, it's probably one of their hubs. Direct flights are common if you're going from one of their hubs to another.

What you should consider before booking

You should consider your **timeline of the trip** in general. Keep in mind that if you want 5 days in Italy, you might need 7 days total for the trip as 2 of them will mostly be eaten up by travel time.

The connection time
Connection time is the amount of time listed that you have from when flight A is supposed to land and Flight B is supposed to board. The site you're booking with will always tell you how much time there is between those two when booking a flight with a connection.

Domestic - I'd recommend no less than 45 mins in the summer for most airports, a half-hour for really small airports (local city airports with only a handful of terminals). In the winter, that's a whole different ball game. So many more things can cause changes or delays in the winter like bad weather in the area you're trying to fly out of or into, de-icing the plane, de-icing the jetway, etc so you need to give yourself more like an hour at least because they may be more likely to change gates on you. While you should be prepared for delays, you can't expect or rely on them, so there's still a sense of urgency to get to the gate area.

International - Most recommend at least 2 hours, you'll need to navigate a foreign airport and you have no control over how far your gates will be from each other. I've gotten away with 1 hour, but it's not always smart to push it. Just plan on chilling in the airport for a while or running frantically with all your stuff through the crowds. #noshame

Other transportation options. Could you get there by train or bus at roughly the same time? You could fly from Lisbon to Madrid, but you might save a few hundred by exploring other options. We'll talk more about other options soon.

The actual time it takes for the whole airport experience
You have to calculate the time it takes to get to the airport, customs/ TSA line, boarding time, general waiting, flight time, waiting for luggage, getting out of the airport, finding/getting to transportation to your destination. It's much more than "just a 5-hour flight". You can use the airport map (usually on the website or app as well as there in the airport) to help plan your routes.

The Airline
You can book flights with whoever you want, but keep in mind that some have more perks like free carry-on, free checked bag, more legroom, snacks, meals, more lenient change flight fees or policies, better customer service, etc. Cheaper usually means fewer perks (Delta Airlines vs Spirit Airlines), so you get what you pay for.

Also the more established airline is at the airport, the more likely that your flight will be from a centralized gate location in the airport (since they will pay a premium for a better spot). That also means that budget airlines are usually suuuuper far away from everything else and will take longer to get to (important to keep in mind when you have a connection flight).

TravelTip: Being a loyal customer to certain airlines can have perks if you fly enough! Racking up miles with certain airlines can result in free flights down the road, but that's a long term game to play. Do what's best for you.

MONEY SAVER: Have a love/hate relationship with Spirit Airlines like the rest of us? I have a tip that might help. Spirit has a 70-80% coupon code usually quarterly that they don't advertise heavily (because they want your money, duh). But you can go to spirit.com, click Deals at the top towards the right. The details usually look like this:

Use Promo Code "70PCT" To Save On Your Next Flight!

Book By: 11:59 PM EST on June 3, 2021

When you fly Spirit, summer fun is just a low fare away

- 70%* off flight-only bookings or the flight portion of vacation packages
- 6/5/21- 6/26/21 (Tues/Wed/Sat Only)
- Enter **70PCT** (all caps, no spaces) in the Promotion Code box on the home page

Please note that coupon only applies to itineraries and the flight portion of a vacation package. Please note that the value of the coupon does not apply to the Passenger Usage Charge (up to $22.99 per segment), Regulatory Compliance Charge (up to $7.00 per segment) or the Fuel Charge (up to $12.00 per segment) which are included in the 'Base Fare'. The coupon will apply to the remaining balance once these are deducted from the combination of the 'Base Fare' and 'Fuel' (where applicable). Additional terms apply. Baggage charges may apply.

Be sure to make sure you continuously plug that code in for every search! It will default without it, because they're sneaky like that.

TIPS WHEN BOOKING

1. Look at flights on your site of choice (more on that below) and compare the best-looking ones to the prices on that airline's direct site. It might be cheaper to book directly through the airline themselves, although usually, it's the same.
2. ALWAYS search for coupon codes. Not all airlines allow these, but budget airlines usually have deals or codes every couple of months. If you see a coupon box, try searching for a code.
3. Be aware that some sites charge a percentage on top of your flight price, so always look at a few different sites until you find one that you trust (and still check the airline site directly).
4. Don't look at prices again once you've booked. It's a painful game to play if you see that prices went down, so just save yourself the pain and don't do it. It's a sunk cost.
5. Consider loyalty to an airline. Your home airport might be a hub to a major airline and banking up miles with them might be beneficial in the long run. If you don't plan on flying frequently, then just go with the cheapest and most convenient flight.
6. Check out the nearby airports. Nearby to your home as well as to your destination. It may not always be a better deal, but sometimes you might get lucky. It's worth the extra 5-10 minutes. Most sites will have a drop-down when you type in a city to provide the airports in that area, click around. Other sites might default to the biggest airport automatically. A quick google search of "insert city" airports will get you a list of your options.
7. Always consider the trade-offs. Saving 20 dollars is not worth the extra layover, but saving $300 might be. There's always a cost involved, but sometimes that cost is your time or convenience, not necessarily your money.

8. Layover airports matter. Consider the issues you might encounter with certain airports that your layover might be in. Having 30 mins to make your connecting flight in O'hare (Chicago) is not enough time to be confident in booking it. Big airports take longer to get around, therefore usually need more time. Smaller airports might not have any food options open so you might need to be prepared with snacks or a small meal.

<u>Sites to book flights on</u>

I use Google Flights. It shows you a bunch of airline options, the price grid shows you the prices on days around the ones you chose, and it never bombards you with ads like other sites do. There are alternatives though like Skyscanner and Momondo as well as others. I haven't seen much success with the sites that claim to give you the secret deals. I do enjoy Dollar Flight Club, though. Expedia and Booking.com are similar but I tend to be overwhelmed by them and largely stick with Google Flights. I might cross reference the flight cost on the direct airline's site once I narrow down what I'm looking for, it's 9 times out of 10 the exact same price, but direct sites sometimes have deals you can grab, like the Spirit code I mentioned previously.

FOR MY NEWBIES:

Okay y'all, I'm going to get really detailed about the airport now, so all my peeps that are comfortable with airports and their processes, feel free to skim the headlines to see what might be useful to you and skip the rest. For all those that are new to the airport scene, no judgment here! We all have our first time at some point, don't worry about it. My goal here is to explain some of the experiences so you can have an idea of what you'll go through. It may feel like everyone around you knows exactly what they're doing and you're a lost duckling, but trust me, most people just have good poker faces. Nine times out of ten, no one will be paying attention to you at all. To pass the time, I'm usually looking for the 3 P's: pizza, (cute) pilots, and puppies! These always made me feel better when I was feeling overwhelmed.

AIRPORT BASICS CHECKLIST

What to do at your home airport:
- Check-in before you arrive (up to 24hours in advance)
- Drop off any checked bags at the baggage stations of your airline (usually what to walk into first at the airport), not applicable if you only have carry-on
- Make your way through security, prepared with a liquid bag and laptops and tablets out and water bottles emptied before getting to the front of the line.
- Walk to your gate
- Get any snacks or food you'll want, refill your water bottle
- Verify you have seat assignment (talk to the attendant, if not)
- Board the plane

What to do after you arrive in the destination airport:
- Fill out the customs form (if international flight)
- Gather all things and deboard the plane
- Head to connecting flight by following the gate signs OR head towards baggage claim to exit the airport
- Go through customs (international flight)
- Continue towards baggage claim (wait for bags, find them, then proceed)
- Head towards transportation
    - Ground transportation = ride-sharing services (Uber, Lyft, taxi, bus, shuttles, etc)
    - Train = often has a certain name that usually has the word *rail, line, or link* in it (Ex: Seattle Tacoma Airport's train is called "Link light rail" so follow signs for that)
    - Order your ticket or ride and wait in the designated area for that transportation
- Exit the airport

Arriving at the airport
There are a few things that might help my newbies out there.
Scared of how complicated the airport complex is? Relax and just follow the signs. Every airport has signs posted to direct you, just pay attention and be prepared to change lanes quickly. When someone is dropping you off and you're *arriving* at the airport, you're going to follow the *Departure* lanes (sounds backward at first, I know) because you're departing to go to a different location. If you're driving yourself there, follow the lanes for parking, sometimes referred to as Decks = parking garages. Not sure which terminal to go to once you're on the right path to departures? There are signs on the side of the road that tell you which terminal has which airlines, just look for those or google it, it's likely to be posted online.

Another cool thing is that in the last couple of years, Google Maps has gotten SO much more detailed, so you can put in "North Terminal, DTW Airport" and it will take you right to it. And Uber/Lyfts often have the option to click which airline you're going to. I've had that happen probably 6 or 7 times now in 2019 & 2020. It's only going to get more and more common, I'm sure.

<u>Parking Off-site from the Airport</u>

I hate paying airport parking prices, but sometimes it's too far or inconvenient to ask someone to pick me up or drop me off (especially for how often I fly). So most of the time I use other off-site parking options that are a lot cheaper. I'll be the first to admit that while it's cheaper, it's definitely more of a hassle and takes more time. You often have to book in advance, wait for their transportation to and from the airport, and it's just another logistical thing to have to deal with. Here's how it works: google *insert airport* parking options, shop around for the best fit for you (price, distance, safety, ratings, etc), google for coupon codes(!), be sure to look if they're 24/7 hours if you have any flights early in the morning or late at night, make the reservation, take a picture of any barcodes or info that might help when you arrive.

Then when the time comes for your trip, arrive at the location, you'll probably have to scan your code or press a button for a ticket, or talk to someone at a booth, then park.

TravelTip: Take a picture of where you've parked! Look for any identifying signs, they should all have some system like a sign that has A4, or B3.

Some places have shuttles that come to scoop you up from your car immediately, some have little bus stop-like stations to wait, and others you have to walk into the office. Your email confirmation should tell you what to do. Take a mental note of what the shuttles or vans look like when you return. The driver should ask you what airline you're traveling on and they usually write down where you're parked on a ticket then hand it to you. I recommend taking a picture of that too since it'll be in your bag/wallet floating around your entire trip. Ride the shuttle to the airport and go about your business as usual.

Once you return, again see what your email confirmation says. Sometimes it's a "call this number once you land" or others have routine schedules that they stick to. You'll typically catch the shuttle at the **ground transportation** area, so follow that sign when exiting the airport. Some airports will have signs of where each shuttle has their own spot to show up and others just have open parking spots from them to arrive at. Just like airlines, typically the more expensive shuttles are closer to the airport door, so if you got a budget one, chances are it'll be towards the back of the line. Just sit or stand tight in an area where you have a good view of many of the shuttles and PAY ATTENTION. Some shuttles are very clearly marked and some aren't, remember that mental note of what your shuttle looks like? Perfect, look for that but keep your eyes open just in case. Playing games on your phone can cause you to miss the shuttle as some of them don't stick around very long or they fill up very quickly, especially with larger families. And it's just a good idea to pay attention to your surroundings.

If your shuttle just isn't showing up, call the number on your email confirmation or go back to the site online, some are more helpful than others, but see what you can find out. Be sure to ask what the shuttle looks like and what it says on the side in case it's just not saying the brand name that you booked under. Have your ticket or picture ready, hop on once it's there, give a ticket to the driver, ride the shuttle back, and they'll take you close to your car. It helps if you tell them your make, model, and color. Have your keys ready to go, make your way to the exit and do the reverse of what you did when you arrived, either put the ticket in the machine, talk to the booth attendant, or press the button, whatever that parking lot has. Then make your way home!

As I said, it's cheaper, but it's not easier. So if you're not strapped for cash, definitely weigh the price/convenience of just parking at the airport, but just know that there are more options out there if you look.

Parking at hotels
Another option is a lot of airports have hotels nearby if you have an early or late flight and want to stay nearby before or after your trip. Almost all of them allow you to park while you're gone and have shuttle services. Research what works for you and find out their policy, some have a week for free, some have a short trip policy, do what works best. The rest of the process is pretty similar to what I've described above. Hotels typically (but not always) have better customer service available, but you get what you pay for. Happy parking!

Standby
Feeling spontaneous? It used to be possible to literally show up at the airport with no tickets and buy one there. Be warned though, that's not the case in today's world. Like all things flight-related, there's a lot of factors that are behind the scenes but a couple of main ones are security after 9/11 and airline algorithms. I've never done it personally so I have no personal experience to share here, but I'd like to at some point in my life.

Malaysia

GOING THROUGH SECURITY

Okay, I'll be honest, one of the frequent traveler's pet peeves in airports are the newbies who don't know what they're doing in the security line. But don't worry, I can teach you the ropes so you will slip through like a pro and no one will have to know.

Here's the strategy. Pay attention to the signs, almost all airports tell you what to do or not to do on the signs, so follow suit. When you're getting close to the front of the security line, take out your 1-quart clear bag of liquids,and your laptop or tablet in preparation to put them in the bins. Take off and place in the bins any jackets, belts, hats, often shoes, (glasses are fine to keep on), or other items that TSA might find sketchy; they'll certainly make it known to you. *Some* airports *sometimes* don't ask that you remove your shoes, you never know, so just pay attention to what's going on in front of you. You'll need to put your phone in the bins and often your passport and tickets as well. Usually, your carry-on bag can just be put on the conveyor belt without a bin, but follow suit with what's in front of you. Purses and everything else goes into bins, usually including shoes. You'll have to manually make sure that they get to the part of the belt that's moving before you can walk away, or you'll likely get yelled at by a lovely TSA agent.

A quick note on some items that I've been curious if I'm allowed to bring onto a plane or that you might be wondering about in my *carry on* before:

YES:
- Nail clippers
- Dry shampoo spray (travel-sized under 3.4 oz)
- My own snacks
- Empty water bottles (to fill up after security)
- Hairstyling equipment (straightener, curlers, etc)
- Small common household batteries
- Plants (lol)
- Little alcohol bottles (travel-sized under 3.4 oz)
- Wet wipes/baby wipes (has prompted a bag search at security for me, but still allowed)
- Nail clippers (a good alternative to scissors)
- Baby food (formulas, food, breast milk, etc)

NO:
It's faster if you Google to see all the things not allowed onto planes.
- Knives
- Aerosols (large cans of hair spray, etc)
- Certain batteries
- Other weapons
- etc

Going through the scanners
Once your items are all in the bins appropriately, you'll need to step in line to go through the scanners. Make sure not to cut anyone in line, there's often one human scanner line for every two baggage scanner lines. Wait in that line, then wait a few feet away from the scanner until the TSA agent waves you forward. There are typically three types of scanners: the typical metal detector-looking kind that's kind of like a doorway, the full-body 360 scanners with air, and one without. The first is super common so you've probably seen it before, but I'll describe the kind without air first.

It's usually a giant glass tube-looking thing that has an opening, you step inside it, place your feet on the shoe prints or other markers, put your arms up like you're doing a jumping jack, and stay still for about 3-7 seconds. The "tube" is about 4 feet in diameter and has a vertical bar that will swivel around you within its glass casing, taking a scan of you just searching for metallic or "potentially harmful" items like explosives. It cannot see you naked.

The final scanner, with air, is the same structure and process as the previously mentioned one, it just shoots puffs of air at you instead of the swiveling bar.

Regardless of the type of scanner, you'll know you're good to go once the TSA agent again waves you forward or tells you you're all set. Proceed to wait for your luggage to pass through the scanners, grab your stuff, and be on your merry way.

If you get stopped by TSA for a further search, they'll likely either ask you to do the scanner again and if it's tripped again they'll likely say something like "Do you have any unidentified objects on you that I should be aware of?", "Sir/Ma'am, I'll have to search you now. I'm going to start by placing my hands ___. " They'll likely either pat search you or use a wand to scan you again in closer proximity. If you've got any metal from surgeries inside your body, it'd be beneficial to mention that but I'm pretty sure the materials that they use in surgeries now aren't designed to set off these types of scanners. If you're not up to anything shady, it's usually just a forgotten piece of jewelry or hairpiece and they'll let you go.

If your bag gets identified for further search, it'll probably go a little something like this. They'll ask whose piece of baggage is in question, you'll raise your hand, they'll wave you over to a search station like 5 feet away. They'll ask if there's anything sharp that they should be aware of, you'll say if there is or not. They'll say they have to open your bag/purse/etc, and they'll use their gloved hands to pull a few things out and poke around in your bag. They'll typically have an idea of what they're looking for from their scanners so they may ask you more direct questions related to what they found concerning. If it's something you're allowed to have, they'll find it, say you're good to go and let you pack your stuff back up and leave. If you have something that is not allowed (for whatever reason), it's really up to that airport and how much of a bad mood the TSA agent is in as to what will happen next. If it's just something like a liquid item in a higher quantity than allowed, they'll probably throw it away in front of you. If it's something illegal, you'll likely have to go in some back room and sign over the item and get a stern talking to as well as whatever legal action is called for in that country. Don't do anything shady and you'll be fine!

Some agents and countries are just much more strict about certain things. One time a very annoyed airport agent in Thailand made a whole scene by taking each and every item out of my liquid bag until she found my toothpaste. It was a normal-sized tube that only had ⅓ left. I'd gotten away with it in like 6 countries by then, but she put up a big fuss because the listed ounces on the tube said more than the allowed 3.4oz. So, she explained to me that she'd have to throw it away, to which I put up no argument, and she proceeded to squeeze the remaining toothpaste into the trash in front of me and then the tube with it. If you can't tell, I'm still pretty salty about how long she held me up over toothpaste, but it just goes to show that you never know what's going to happen. Just stay calm and reasonable, and you'll be fine. You can probably buy more of whatever the issue was pretty easily anyways or live without it for a little while.

What is the deal with this TSA Precheck?

TSA Precheck is kind of like paying for the US to do a background check on you so when you pass the background check, you can get special treatment at US Airports. It's a program to identify low-risk travelers to expedite the screening process (aka. security). So while it wasn't going to be any good for me outside of the US, I wanted the perks. It's good for 5 years, and here's what you get:

Passengers no longer have to remove shoes*, the 3-1-1 liquid compliant bag, laptops*, light outerwear/jackets, and belts* and get to go through the Precheck line (with typically only 5-minute waits). Though these passengers are still subject to random searches, the overall process tends to go by much more quickly. *https://www.tsa.gov/precheck*

While I find Precheck to be awesome for me, I wouldn't recommend it unless you fly around the US very often. The only 2 major drawbacks I've seen of Precheck is that it sucks if I'm traveling with someone who doesn't have it, so I usually choose to wait in line with them anyways but then I don't have to take my liquids out or my shoes off as often. The other is that #COVID has pretty much shut down any precheck line from being open because it requires more staffing that airports just aren't deciding to do.

Somewhere over the Southwest USA 2021

General Airport Tips

1. TRAVEL LIGHT. I'll speak more on this later, but it's pretty self-explanatory, the less you bring, the less you have to deal with lugging around. Even though you can send off your checked luggage when you walk into the airport, you still have to haul it in, pick it up, and lug it to your destination. Whenever possible I would recommend you travel with only a carry-on. It's so much easier.
2. I also prefer using backpacks or my hiking pack (Carry on size) over rolling suitcases. I like being able to move swiftly as one unit with my items on my back rather than dragging around a suitcase that falls over, gets caught, causes a racket on any non-flat surface. (You should hear how obnoxious suitcases are on cobblestone) Backpacks also distribute the weight more evenly than duffle bags. That gets old, very quickly. This again is a personal preference, but you do you. Just consider all your options.
3. What should you put in your carry-on? Must-haves like medicines, toiletries, and a few outfits can hold you over in the event that your luggage gets lost. Snacks and chargers are important too.
4. Check out the airport map beforehand to get a general idea of the layout. It'll make things a lot easier, especially in big airports that you aren't familiar with. Maps are usually posted throughout the airport or on the airport website. They aren't required but could ease some anxiety for my fellow anxious travelers.
5. Don't show up with full water bottles or drinks. You cannot make it through TSA with that liquid so either chug before you get to the front of the line or dump it in a water fountain prior to getting in the security check line.

General Airplane Tips

I've been on over 100 flights at this point, so here are a few things that I've learned that work for me along the way.

1. If you plan on watching movies on the plane, always have headphones that have the aux cord connection so they will plug into the TV on the seat in front of you and you won't have to wait for the half-hour before they start handing them out after take off. This is also good for laptops while waiting in the airport.
2. Blanket scarves. I'm always cold (it's just who I am as a person) but even if you're not, you never know what the temperature will be on the plane (it can go to both extremes on the same flight). It makes a great pillow for napping if you don't want to wear it. Most fold down pretty well when you roll them.
3. I don't use neck pillows since they usually would take up too much space in my little backpack or my hiking pack, but others enjoy having them. Up to you, pal!
4. Travel with a little hand sanitizer (under 3.4 fluid oz, of course). They're handing little individual pouches of them out now in 2020 because of #covid19. It'll lessen your chances of getting sick while traveling!

5. Download some music or movies. I'm all about that Offline mode on Spotify! Download playlists or artists when you have wifi and you'll have music wherever you go. Netflix, Hulu, Apple TV, Disney+, and Amazon Prime apps all allow you to download certain shows and movies for offline use. They do expire at different times though, so be sure to do it close to when you're ready to leave. Some only stay on your device for 7 days.

6. All about that sleep mask. I enjoy the darkness when I'm trying to sleep so my super tiny sleep mask is awesome for when that person across the aisle from you decides to be the only person on the plane letting in the blinding light straight into your eyes.

7. Bring snacks from home and an empty water bottle. Tons of flights give out some sort of snacks (not Spirit, lol) but they're super small and not necessarily something you like. Bring a little somethin'-somethin' to eat while you're strapped into your seat for hours. Be mindful of how crunchy or smelly your snack is. Beef jerky will make the 20+ feet around you smell like nothing but that and that might not *fly* well with your fellow passengers. #pun

8. Lots of people like gum to chew to help with the ear-popping sensation when you're adjusting to the pressure changes. Even fake chewing helps sometimes.

9. Chapstick and neutral smelling hand lotion is a great idea to have in your personal item. Airplane air filtration systems are great but can seriously dry your skin and lips out quickly. Stay hydrated too!

10. Chill out when the plane lands, you're not going to be able to get off immediately so just sit tight until about 5 rows in front of you have exited. Then gather all your belongings and make your way off.

11. Have a pen with you for the customs declaration form. Otherwise, you'll be pushed to the back of the line since you'll have to find one to fill out the form before you get in line.

12. Please, please! Never clap when the plane lands.

Fun fact: Confused where the 3.4 fluid oz comes from for the accepted rate of liquids in your carry-on? It's 3.4 fluid oz because that is 100 mLs. (Can't wait for the US to go metric) #Metricsystem

Snack services

I feel like peanuts are such a cliche of a plane snack in movies but I can't recall a single time I've been served peanuts. It's usually almonds. Anyways, budget airlines (think Spirit, Allegiant, RyanAir, AirAsia) usually won't serve you anything for free, but you can buy all sorts of stuff including alcohol. #expensive

Most other airlines you'll recognize will provide you a snack and a soft beverage (some will offer wine or beer for free) if it's more than an hour flight. Snacks are usually something like crackers, cookies, nuts, trail mix, pretzels, etc in little tiny pouches and sometimes a little water bottle. In 2020, Delta Airlines has sped up that process by handing out preassembled ziplock bags with hand sanitizer, Biscoff cookies, a little water bottle, a napkin, and a sanitizer wipe. I'm assuming other airlines are doing something similar as well.

#TravelTip: Always accept the snack. You may not feel like having it now, but they're small and travel-sized and might help you feel better if you get queasy or might tide you over some other time on your trip. Free snacks are always a good idea. Same with the water bottle if you're traveling to places that you can't drink the tap water. Those are perfect for brushing your teeth, trust me.

Difference between Domestic and International Flights

It may seem like the only difference between Domestic and International flights is that you need a passport to fly abroad, but that's just the tip of the iceberg.

DOMESTIC FLIGHTS	INTERNATIONAL FLIGHTS
Requires US issued photo ID (new requirements coming 2021)	Requires US issued passport, May require a visa to some countries
Have to go through screening checkpoints (TSA security)	Have to go through screening checkpoints (TSA security)
Must comply with airport and airline rules at all times	Have to go through U.S. Customs and Border Protection checks (often referred to as just customs)
	Fill out and submit the Customs Declaration form(upon landing in another country)
	Must comply with airport and airline rules at all times

Let's get down to business on a few things about international airports, shall we?
What does an "International Airport" actually mean? Ex. O'Hare International Airport (Chicago)
Great question - It's pretty simple, even though it may sound like they only do international flights, it actually just means that that airport consistently has international flights arrive and depart. Most of the larger airports have 'international' in their name for that reason, but they still have a plethora of domestic flights. Smaller airports might have international flights but rarely; they focus on more domestic and localized travel.

You'll have to fill out a "customs declaration form" when you travel internationally. It seems scary but in simple terms, it's just the checks and balances for countries to find out what passengers are bringing into their country. It helps to prevent invasive species and protect a variety of things.

What does this mean for you? It means that you'll fill out a form and submit it to the customs agents. If all your answers are No, then they'll likely just stamp it and send you on your way. If you answer yes to anything, they'll likely stop you and ask questions, with the possibility of your luggage getting searched and the item of concern being confiscated. So, if you want a smooth ride, just don't travel with any of the following:

11	I am (We are) bringing		
	(a) fruits, vegetables, plants, seeds, food, insects:	Yes	No
	(b) meats, animals, animal/wildlife products:	Yes	No
	(c) disease agents, cell cultures, snails:	Yes	No
	(d) soil or have been on a farm/ranch/pasture:	Yes	No
12	I have (We have) been in close proximity of **livestock:** (such as touching or handling)	Yes	No
13	I am (We are) carrying **currency or monetary instruments** over $10,000 U.S. or foreign equivalent: (see definition of monetary instruments on reverse)	Yes	No
14	I have (We have) **commercial merchandise:** (articles for sale, samples used for soliciting orders, or goods that are not considered personal effects)	Yes	No

Depending on the airport, sometimes you will submit this ticket to an automated machine that will take your picture and print out a new little slip (like Toronto Pearson International Airport (YYZ) in Toronto, Canada), then you'll take that slip to the "gatekeeper" who will either take it from you and wave you through or ask you to step aside for further inspection. The other possibility is that there are no machines and you just take the form to a gatekeeper and they review it there and either wave you through or ask you to step aside. If you're worried about knowing who to take what to, there are signs everywhere, and the flow of the airport forces you through these checkpoints, so you can't miss them. But you can be prepared for them. Look around you and follow suit.

TransAtlantic or TransPacific Flights
There are a few key differences for flights that cross oceans. For starters, chances are a transatlantic or transpacific flight is going to use the biggest plane you'll ever be on. I'm talking HUGE. 10 seats across (like this -> (XXX| |XXXX| |XXX). 75+ rows. They're usually aon Airbus A330, Boeing 767, Boeing 777, orand Boeing 787., Google them if you're interested. Another difference is that you'll typically be served a meal because the flight is longer. Flight meals are usually interesting and mediocre, but at least they're free and warm. You usually get the option between 2 main courses (vegetarian option if you ask) and everyone gets a tray of the same sides. Your tray will probably have the following: heat-sealed the main course with a warm side included, little plastic containers with another side, a plastic-wrapped bread roll of some form, a desert, cutlery pouch, butter, and a water bottle. They'll also ask what you'd like to drink with the options like water, soda / pop, apple, orange, or grape juice, wine, beer, or ginger ale.

I've been on probably over 100 flights and I still get nervous to talk to the steward for no reason, they're usually nice or at the very least professionally polite. Just go for it.

Airports in other countries

Quick notes about airports outside of the US. No airport is going to be the same, but the general layouts and processes are all pretty similar. All the airports I've been to use a mixture of symbols and languages on their signs so whether you can speak the language or not, you should be able to figure it out. We're extremely fortunate to be English speakers as most airports have their language as primary and most likely English as secondary. You'll always have to check into your flight, go through security, find your gate, etc. However, it might be a bit more confusing the first few times.

When I'm flying domestically, I use the airline app for my tickets, but I highly recommend getting your ticket printed at the kiosk or counter when you fly internationally just so you have something to show that the staff is used to. Your phone may die, glitch, or just not be accepted, you never know. If you have a connection flight, the kiosk should print out both tickets (1 for destination A to B and another for B to C) but there's a chance something will change (the gate, your seat number, the flight time, etc.) **so ALWAYS double-check the screens with the flights for the gate and departure time.** The screens update in real-time, and it takes time to get from one gate to another, so I'd hate for you to miss your flight because of outdated info on your boarding pass. If you have extra time, you can check your seat number by printing the ticket again at the kiosks or counters but that is much less important.

When do you go through customs?
You will go through customs *at your destination airport.* AKA the country you're trying to leave the airport at. That means if I'm flying from the US to Ecuador for vacation, then I'll go through normal airport security in the US, and I'll go through customs once I arrive in Ecuador. When I leave Ecuador, I'll go through normal airport security and once I'm landed in the US, I'll go through customs again. This is because you're going to leave the airport and be within that country's borders. You don't go through customs during your connection flights because you're not trying to leave the airport. That's why there are signs that say "CONNECTIONS"; it keeps you in the airport whereas "Baggage Claim" and "Transportation" takes you down hallways that have checkpoints that say "No return from this point on". They're usually one-lane stalls that you have to pass through that are otherwise very blocked off.

Yes, you have to go through customs to get back into your home country. In my experience, it's no easier/faster to get into your home country than most others. You'll have to go through the same process regardless, it's usually up to the airport processing speed or how many other flights just arrived in addition to yours. There usually is a different line to get into though. It'll say something like "US PASSPORTS" through this line, sometimes it's US and Canadian passports combined. When trying to get into Europe there will be a European Passport line for all citizens of countries in the EU and a non-EU passport line.

What's it like going through customs?
Well, it can be pretty nerve-racking since it feels so official and we're usually pretty clueless on what's going on. But in reality, if you're not doing anything shady, then it's really painless. You wait in line for a while and then the next available attendant will wave you to come to them (or their sign lights up), you hand them your passport, plane ticket, and visa if applicable.

#TravelTip: Have your passport open to the page with your picture and have your ticket on that page as well so they can read it easily.

Some countries will also require you to have proof of when you're leaving, to make sure you're not planning to stay more than the allowed days without a visa. So, if you know that they'll ask, have your departing ticket ready on your phone. Some also want to know what address you'll be staying at during your time in that country.

I usually move around a lot, so there's more than 1 address, but I just give them the address that I can pull up the fastest and not mention the moving around. Don't lie if they ask you, but sometimes the fewer details the better. They'll probably ask you around 3-7 questions, nothing hard to answer. Some might ask you nothing at all, just giving you a cold stare as they match your face to your passport.

Here are some examples of what they might ask:
- What brings you to _____?
- Are you here on business or leisure (to be a tourist or visit friends/family)?
- How long are you staying for?
- Are you meeting anyone here?
- Are you traveling with anyone?
- What are some of your plans while you're in ____?
- Are you planning to travel within the country?
- Where will you be staying?

Here are some normal responses to give to the questions:
- What brings you to _____?
    - "I'm playing tourist" "I'm traveling for a holiday/vacation"
- Are you here on business or leisure (to be a tourist or visit friends/family)?
    - "Leisure"
- How long are you staying for?
    - "I'll be staying for a week then flying back to the US"
- Are you meeting anyone here?
    - "No, just sightseeing." or "Yes, I'm meeting my friend"
- Are you traveling with anyone?
    - "yes, I have my friend/family/coworker with me"
- What are some of your plans while you're in ____?
    - "I want to see the Eiffel Tower"
- Are you planning to travel within the country?
- "No, just staying in Paris" or "Yes, my next destination is Bordeaux"
- Where will you be staying?
    - "I've got an Airbnb booked for my stay"

After questioning, customs will scan your passport and once they're satisfied, they'll (usually) stamp your passport and hand your documents back, and you proceed through the area. It's important to note that not all countries will stamp your passport, but it is still a common practice despite everything being recorded digitally.

Some airports have added security, like requiring your picture to be taken without hats, glasses, or other face obstructions. Other airports require fingerprint scanning from only 1 to all your fingers. Be prepared for anything!

I haven't been to Russia or China (I avoid connections there just because they're likely to be more of a hassle) so I can't speak to what those processes are like.

If thinking about going through security makes you anxious, just believe me when I say that nothing terrible will happen and they'll never remember you specifically, so just breathe and try to be as prepared as you can. Trust me, I've said some really stupid stuff to custom agents because I was either sleep deprived or just misunderstood the question or just me being me. They just laughed me off and sent me on my way. Even if they're rude or cold, they're just doing their job and you're just trying to see the world. Don't waste mental energy on it.

Difference between the European Union and Schengen Area
Honestly, I don't think I'd be able to explain well what the Schengen Area is compared to the EU. Basically though, it's an area that allows the movement of people with less restrictions between the borders of the participating countries. Entering and leaving the area come with more security checks, and less when you travel within the area.

Key Takeaways of International Airports

- Research what documents you'll need for each country
- Have your passport open and ready with your ticket (and visa if applicable)
- Look around you and follow along
- Have a pen on you
- Relax and don't stress about it

Motion Sickness:
I don't know about you, but I get motion sickness super easily. My tips to those who are unfortunately with me on that would be:
1. Always have something in your stomach and a neutral snack on hand.
2. Be wary of having subtitles on. They trigger me when it's a bumpy ride.
3. Take deep and consistent breaths. See if you can gently burp (not barf).
4. Sleep as much as possible (can't get super sick if you're not conscious).
5. Position yourself to move with the turbulence forward-backward, not side-to-side. Side to side immediately sends me into a tailspin, but I've learned how to adjust myself to avoid as much as possible.
6. Close your eyes and picture something that can't move. Like a big beautiful tree in a summer field or a beautiful sunset. I know it's hard, but just try not to think about actually being sick, just think about when you'll feel normal again.
7. Ginger Ale can help if it's available as an option.

<u>Medicine for motion sickness:</u>
Dramamine is available over the counter (comes in form of two active ingredients: either dimenhydrinate= drowsy*, or meclizine = less drowsy). If you get the chance to purchase meds in other countries where dispensing laws are more lax (certain things in other countries may be available without a prescription), consider picking up Zofran (ondansetron generic name), a scopolamine patch, or Vistaril (hydroxyzine pamoate) from a pharmacy. *not pharmacist recommended* **Do your research and consult your doctors before traveling.**

Ordering Ride Sharing Services to leave the airport

The process to order ride-sharing services is different at every airport and I find that it's continually evolving, so bear with me as I can only tell you what I've seen so far.

The bottom line is that the ride-sharing apps (Lyft, Uber, etc) have included zones to choose from when you get to the checkout screen, there are drop-down options to choose from. In my experience, what's on the app does not always match what's on signs around you, so don't panic and just try to pick the closest marker to your blue pin location.

Also don't panic if you have to walk quite a ways across parking lots or down corridors to follow the rideshare signs, because airports were built way before ride-sharing was a thing so they've had to figure out where to make that space to keep everyone safe and separate.

In Austin, Texas, there was a designated ride-sharing spot in a parking garage with a specific attendant that stood there and asked for your 4 digit code and put you in the driver first in line, so you didn't know who was assigned to you until that driver put in that 4 digit code to see where they were taking you. Strange, but it worked out fine.

In Atlanta, Georgia, it's a huge airport so I did my best to pick the right pick-up point out of the 15+ options but the signs didn't match anything I had to choose from. The driver ended up having to call me and I described what I saw around me. Luckily this wasn't his first rodeo, so he took what I said and tried a different area where we eventually found each other.

In Fort Lauderdale, Florida, no Lyfts or Ubers were accepting my ride request at all, so we eventually just went the taxi route. For that, we only had to walk to this little stand where a dude with a walkie-talkie was standing and he got us in the next taxi.

In San Juan, Puerto Rico, it was super easy and everything matched perfectly and the ride only cost 17 dollars to downtown San Juan. Throwing that in there to show sometimes it's really easy and cheap. (:

GENERAL Q&A

- **What if I lose my ticket? -** Go to the kiosk or desk. If you're through security already, your airline rep at the gate should be able to help.

- **Why did my name get called on the PA system? -** You're probably late for your flight and they're doing the last boarding or you left an item somewhere.

- **Why did they call me up to the podium at my gate? -** It's probably a seat change or you're in an emergency exit row and need your verbal approval.

- **Why do they need my approval in an emergency exit row? -** There's a law that flight attendants must confirm with the people in emergency exit rows (the window that would open into a door) that they are willing and able to help in the case of an emergency landing. You must verbally say "yes" or "I will" or some sort of verbal confirmation. It's a nice bonus for taller individuals as there's waaaay more legroom for no extra charge.

- **Can I ask to have my seat changed? -** You can ask, but it's up to the attendants if they'll accommodate you. You can also ask fellow passengers if they're willing to switch with you. Chances are you'll have to wait until the boarding ends before they'll do anything.

- **I'm scared to go potty on the plane, what do I do? -** I feel ya, I didn't go potty on a plane until I was like 100 flights in because I was too scared. Just get over it and go. It's a cramped little room but no one will hear anything you do. The walk is good for you anyways.

- **Can I grab something out of my luggage up in the stowaway?** - Of course, just be mindful of others as stuff could fall out when you open it or when you open your bag. I wouldn't do it unless it's reeeeally important to you or no one else is around you.

- **Can I choose my seat? -** Sometimes when you check-in, you can choose your seat. On some airlines, it's an added cost (budget airlines) but others are free *within* your type of ticket (economy, business class, 1st class). Look for a "View/change seat assignment" option, typically it's easier on a desktop or the airline app. Online on your mobile device might not show that option.

- **When's the best time to check-in? -** Typically you can check in 24-36 hours before your flight departure time. I've got no confirmation on this, but I'm getting the suspicion that they auto-assign seats as passengers check-in from the back of the plane to the front. I'm usually very eager to check in as soon as I can because of the type of person that I am, but I'm often put waaaay in the back of the plane. Coincidence? I think not. I'd recommend any time between 6-12 hours before your flight. It might give you a better row assignment (if it is back-to-front assignments) or the chance to still have good seats to choose from if you do have the change seat option.

- **Should I bring my own food or eat at the airport?** - Up to you. When I was on a tight budget, I wouldn't dare eat at the airport. It's not always crazy expensive, but it can be and every penny adds up. It's typically like convenience store prices, definitely not cheap affordable food or snacks. But if it's worth it to you to feel full, kill time, and save the snack prepping for another time, then by all means go for it.

ACCOMMODATIONS

You've got to sleep somewhere, so let's dive into accommodations. There are tons of options of places to stay with an insane range from just a bunk bed to a full house with infinity pools and even yachts! #insane

As a general rule for booking hotels/resorts that are listed on multiple sites, check the sites like Booking.com or Expedia.com and compare their prices to the direct hotel or resort site. They often have different prices or promos going on.

There are Google Chrome extensions that might help show you prices listed on different sites like Honey. There are tons of sites that claim to provide you with the best deals, but personally, I've never seen one be any better than others consistently: Expedia, Booking, Groupon, Kayak, Travelocity, Trivago, etc. Some of them offer points when you book through them, so loyalty might eventually add up, but it takes time and a lot of booking to become worthwhile. Also beware that sometimes it's more complicated to change or cancel bookings when it's through 3rd party sites, so do your research if that's a concern.

My advice for looking for picking where to stay would be to remember that while it may be tempting to pay the extra few bucks for the fancier place or the one with more bells and whistles, remember it's essentially just a place for you to sleep and store your belongings for a while. If you want the bells and whistles, go for it! Especially on trips to all-inclusive resorts where that's where you'll be spending a majority of your time.

Just be wary that accommodation is going to be a huge portion of your trip expenses and you might be asleep most of the time you're there. I'd advise you to stay towards the cheaper or more convenient options than the cute or plush options. I find that you'll be remembering more about what you are going out to do during the day/evening than the place you stayed. However, find the line between cheap and safe; it's often the case that the cluster of suuuper cheap places might be that price because of the neighborhood they're in. Do your research and read the comments/reviews.

There are certainly some exceptions that we'll mention below, so let's get into it!

Here's a break down of the more common types of places to stay:

Hotels

You've heard of a hotel before, I'm sure. They're everywhere with their own range of quality and amenities. You pay the nightly rate and get your own room with access to what amenities they have onsite like pools, hot tubs, business centers, etc. Some get super fancy with huge lobbies that have two-story waterfalls or mini shopping malls for the main floor and others are just the bare bones of rooms to sleep and a table with a coffee machine.

Just shop around until you find a hotel that meets your needs in terms of location, if they have shuttles to/ from the airport, and the cost. Remember that while it may be tempting to pay the extra few bucks for the fancier hotel or the bigger room with the King bed, it's essentially just a place for you to sleep. I typically go for 2-3 star hotels as long as their reviews aren't terrible. Most are just standard rooms, nothing special but it allows me to save some money for more fun things!

I'd recommend signing up for the rewards programs of the bigger chains if you think there's any possibility of multiple times you'll stay in hotels. Pick a generic hotel password and use it for all the chains. Get whatever member discounts they offer for signing up and then immediately unsubscribe on the first email you get from them.

Also be sure to think about any memberships you may have that offer partnership discounts such as AAA, Groupon, and credit card rewards; they often have links to book through or discount codes. Google that hotel and type in coupon code before you check out to see if there are any deals online that you should be aware of!

Airbnb

Airbnb has grown incredibly fast since I started traveling, there are more options than ever before! You can find anything from a single room and bathroom to an entire house or condo.

Ask your friends if they have an account before you sign up so they can send you a referral link. They'll get some free credits out of it! It'll take some time and effort to sign up, but it's so worth it, in my opinion. Airbnb's are my favorite and usually the first place I check when I begin to look at accommodations. They'll need some information to create a secure account to add a layer of security for the renters who are allowing people into their homes/ on their property, but it's a simple process.

The app is very easy to use and continuously improving as is the website. They are also expanding their experience section as well as places to stay! Check those out too!

The typical process would be that you find the place you like, you try to book it (some are instant, others need to be approved by hosts), then you get confirmation that it's booked. Once booked, you get a message from the host with any specific details like the address, where to park, how to enter, codes to get inside, details of the place, recommendations of the area, etc. You're able to message back and forth with the host to figure out any other details needed, like early or late check-in times, for example. You stay at their place, then you leave! No real check-out like a hotel. Then you'll get an email asking you to review the place and the features available to make sure the listing is accurate, and you can leave reviews for others looking at booking the place! The hosts will also have the opportunity to review you as a guest for other hosts who decide whether to accept your requests or not. You cannot see what they wrote about you until you review them and vice versa so it can't be as biased. So yes, you as a guest will have a rating as well, so don't trash the place or disturb the neighbors or you might not be allowed in other listings on the site.

Airbnb does look at "certain databases of public state and county criminal records, as well as state and national sex offender registries for criminal convictions and sex offender registrations" when hosts try to make accounts, if you're concerned about safety.

I've had nothing but pleasant experiences on Airbnb except a mix-up of information one time on where to find the key to get in while I was in Thailand. Airbnb listings have allowed me to stay in places that I would have never had the chance to otherwise like two apartment buildings with infinity pools on the roof! #awesome

So if you're comfortable with staying on someone else's property, give it a shot! There are so many amazing options all over the world. Remember though that this is someone's property, so please treat it with respect.

Vrbo

Vrbo is very similar to Airbnb so most of the same information applies, but I've found Vrbo to have found a niche in longer rentals (think multiple weeks vs only a few days). Vrbo and Airbnb might have the same listing (place) but there's often a price difference. I've been finding that Airbnb has been a bit more expensive in most cases, but not all. It's probably because Airbnb has more name recognition and users, but that's just my speculation. The process is basically the same in terms of booking.

There are different options the host can choose in terms of what you need to pay upfront in order to book, some require nothing and others require all of it. There are tons of options in between too, all up to the host. There are also differing refund policies for canceling, so be sure to know what you're signing up for. Check out their policy page for more information.

In my experience, I booked with Vrbo only once for my 5 weeks stay in Puerto Rico and Vrbo had a better discount for long stays (over 28 days) than the same listings did on Airbnb. I paid 60% upfront on the policy of full refund if I canceled 35 days before the date of my arrival. For longer stays and putting that much money down, it made me feel better to communicate directly with the property manager through the "contact the property manager" button. It was only about 5 emails back and forth, but it allowed me to see his response time, how he answered my questions and general feel for how he manages. The stay is scheduled for about 8 months from now because I wanted to make sure no one would book a single weekend, preventing me from having the space for the full 5 weeks. So I'll provide an update on this book with any lessons learned once that happens. **Follow my Instagram @hali.motley for my Puerto Rico journey!**

Hostels

Ahhh, hostels. One of the first things I think of when I hear "backpacking around Europe" is hostels. I've had tons of great experiences in hostels in Europe and Southeast Asia.

You're mostly going to find hostels in major cities, and trust me there are TONS. They're much more popular in Europe, South America, and Asia than they are in the US. They're perfect for a cheap place to sleep and store your belongings while you travel during the day. They're also a hotspot for meeting fellow young travelers and making new friends. At as cheap as $10-$25/night, they're usually found right in the center of things, close to the action and high energy. It's amazing the cool themes and features some of them have, too. Hostels are an amazing chance to stay at some amazing places for really cheap. Some have pools or rooftop bars, awesome lounges, cute bathrooms, all sorts of charm, and awesome kitchens.

The biggest draw for hostels is the chance to meet fellow travelers! It's amazing the people you can meet and the stories they have to share. While you don't have to talk to anyone, the overall vibe is that everyone is open to meeting new people, so starting conversations is extremely easy. Lucky for my introverted self, tons of people came up to me or my BFF first so I didn't have to have the anxiety of striking up a conversation.

The hands-down best site to use when looking at hostels is HostelWorld. It's a lot like Airbnb in terms of the setup, with tons of listings that have pictures, descriptions, and reviews from previous guests. It's incredibly user-friendly and the app is amazing as well. It's recommended to book online rather than just showing up, but I don't think they'd turn you away if they have open rooms.

Some listings show a breakdown of who is booked to stay there on the same dates that you're looking for which is so awesome! So you can see how many English speakers are staying and all the nationalities of the guests (not names or info, just number of guests).

What I pay attention to most when looking at listings:
- Free wifi
- Food options (if breakfast is included or if there's restaurant inside)
- Cool common areas to meet people
- Reviews (especially from other young women for my peace of mind)
- Distance to my activities or transportation hubs (bus or train stations, etc)
- Safety of neighborhood

General notes about Hostels:

Tons of hostels have partnerships with bars, restaurants, or tourist services near them to provide discounts, coupons, or special happy hours, so be sure to look out for those!

The cheapest rates you'll get will be for a single bed in a larger room, the smaller the number of people in a room, usually, the more the price goes up. Not by much usually, just a couple of dollars. You can usually choose between co-ed, male-only, or female-only rooms. I usually aim for rooms with less than 12 people, defaulting to female-only when it's available. I have slept in co-ed plenty of times with no issues other than the general noise of people being around.

The general rule is that if you're in the sleeping rooms, it's to be quiet and there are usually "sleeping hours" to respect. Luckily there are almost always other areas specifically designed to hang out and be around people so you can be there as long as you want.

Also, some hostels have specific hours that you can come and go as you please, but after that point, they'll be locking the doors for safety. It's usually posted all over the place, so just pay attention if you plan on having a late night.

Depending on the experience you want, the comments and rankings on HostelWorld will let you know super easily if it's a party hostel or has chill vibes for just a safe place to sleep. Choose what's right for you at the time you need it, if you know you'll need a day of rest after traveling a lot, just find a quieter-looking hostel. There's something for everyone!

Most hostels are for people 18-30. For my fellow 20-somethings out there, no problemo, so it's not something you really have to look out for. Some allow younger than 16, but you'll have to dig more and there are some that allow 30+.

I asked my mom to go to Europe with me when I was presenting a paper at Oxford University in 2017 but on one condition. She had to travel how I travel: backpacking style. To my delight, she was fully on board and kept up with me the entire time, including a stay at a hostel in Paris. It took some searching for a hostel that allowed 30+ in the arrondissement that I wanted us to stay in, but I found several with good reviews and she ended up having a blast. So if you have parents that are nervous when you tell them you want to stay at hostels, just tell them that Hali's mom is awesome and approves of them! (;

The chill area of a hostel in Dublin, Ireland

CouchSurfing

If you're really on a budget and like to meet people, consider using CouchSurfing.com
The main draw for most people, I believe, is that most of the hosts on the site are or were travelers themselves, so there's a level of mutual understanding and interest in travel.

This is probably the riskiest of all the options I've listed, but it's still a fine option nonetheless. Know your limits, trust your instinct, and have a backup plan.

I've never used CouchSurfing, so I can't speak to it personally, but there's a lot of information online if you're interested! I know quite a few people who have used it and enjoyed their experiences!

Resorts

Resorts are definitely not in the category of "just a place to sleep". They also have a huge range of options from Ski resorts to Beach resorts, small to large, all-inclusive to full-on waterparks.

Most people who book resorts are typically going to spend a majority of their time in the resort itself because resorts are designed to have a ton of activities and amenities. They usually have full restaurants, pools, hot tubs, casinos, some sort of natural attraction like being right on the ocean or in the mountains. Some are designed for families, others are adult-only, and some are all-inclusive. All-inclusive means that you pay a flat rate for accommodation and access to everything on site such as unlimited drinks and food, access to lounges, pools, activities, etc.

Resorts are perfect if you want to show up and have all the fun at your fingertips without having to coordinate getting around to everything. However, most resorts do have partnerships with local excursions to activities in the area.

These are very popular on the tropical coasts like Cancun, Mexico, for example. You're definitely paying for the convenience of everything, but it's just simplified by being a flat upfront fee.

There are a ton of different resort chains, so decide where you want to go then look at your different options. Be sure to check out Groupon for special deals, there's usually a ton! Read the reviews, as always.

When you Google resorts in the location that you decide, there'll be a ton of sites like Expedia and Booking.com that will have options, but always be sure to compare those prices to those on the direct site of the resort. Sometimes there are special offers or chances to upgrade for the same price by booking directly.

#TravelTip: remember to take at least $100 worth of ones and 5s when going to All-inclusive resorts to tip the staff that you interact with. It's not easy to break large bills so come prepared with small bills specifically for tipping.

Safety

Like most things in today's tech world, you can vet the place before you book or show up there, and if a place is giving you a bad feeling online or in person, just don't go there and find someplace new. Pictures and others reviews are your best friend when it comes to checking a place out before you commit to it, so take advantage of those resources.

If you're ever concerned about something, speak up or take action. If that action is getting out of there and just eating the cost, then so be it. Your peace of mind and safety are more important.

Key Takeaways of ACCOMMODATIONS

- Remember that it's mostly a place to sleep, don't overpay
- Explore your options on different platforms before deciding, shop around
- Check for discount codes online before you check out
- Ask your friends for referral codes before you create accounts

	Pro	Con	Best for
Hotel	- Available in all tourist areas -Pretty standard expectations -Room to yourself -Might have a pool/hot tub (In the US mostly) -staff on-site for help/guidance	-On the expensive side from overhead costs -can be boring comparatively	Families or small groups
Airbnb	-More homey/ authentic experience -listings can have awesome advantages (be on the lake, hot tub, great view, etc) -Some hosts on-site to help/guide, add to the experience -location can be amazing	-Cost varies extremely, service and cleaning fees can add up a lot -sometimes you don't want a host on-site -can be harder to get to sometimes, less desirable locations	Varies extremely. Could be huge property for housing a large group to one person just renting a single bedroom
Vrbo	-Similar to Airbnb -Directed towards longer rentals, higher discounts for 28+ days -Properties can be once in a lifetime stays -location can be amazing	-Cost varies extremely, service and cleaning fees can add up a lot -sometimes you don't want a host on-site -can be harder to get to sometimes, less desirable locations	Varies extremely. Could be huge property for housing a large group to one person just renting a single bedroom
Hostel	-Cheap options in the heart of cities -opportunity to meet fellow travelers -cool vibes and experiences	-less privacy -often shared bathrooms -noise level is higher -less predictable	Solo or two travelers on a budget looking to meet people
CouchSurfing	-Cheapest option -Unique experience -get to meet hosts	-less predictable -higher uncertainty	Budget travelers

Resorts	-Tons of activities on site	-usually very expensive	Families, couples, groups that are looking for a more stress-free vacation with fewer moving pieces, preferring to enjoy the amenities on site
	-typically the highest level of customer service	-experience can depend on other guests behavior	
	-opportunity to meet fellow guests	-often crowds of very drunk people	
	-opportunity to pick the style that fits you best		

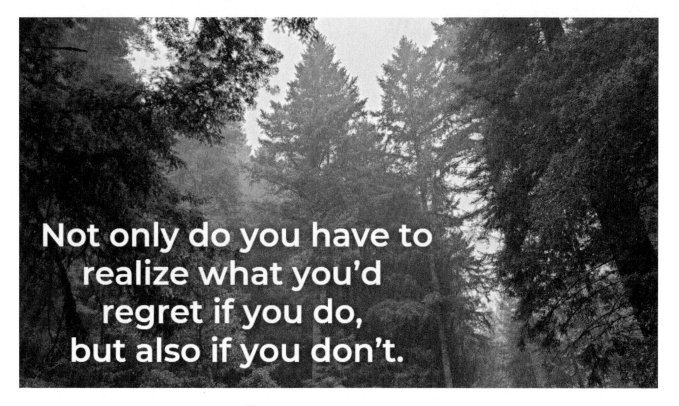

Transportation

Time to make John Candy and Steve Martin proud and talk about Planes, Trains, and Automobiles (1987 movie reference). Since you've decided on the locations you'd like to try to go to, the next step is seeing how to get there.

Depending on where you're coming from, different types of transport might be more or less advantageous. Obviously, planes are useful for crossing oceans or seas, or just really long distances. Trains are great for fairly long distances across countries or continents. Buses are great for going between nearby cities but can also get you across the country fairly commonly. Cars are great for getting you around cities or between close by towns. Boats or ferries are perfect for island hopping or getting from one side of the bay or gulf to the other.

Important note that **you should practice caution from pickpocketing at all times, be on EXTRA high alert at transportation stations**. These areas are a pickpocket's dream because there's usually a ton of moving people who are packed close together, people are distracted trying to navigate to where they need to go, and there are tons of tourists.

- Hold your bags in front of you, use mini locks, and keep valuables where you can feel them like front pockets or in secret fanny pack belts.
- Avoid keeping your phone or wallet in your backpacker or having bags or purses that don't have a way to seal in some way.
- Be suspicious of people bumping into you or causing scenes, they're skilled at drawing your attention to where they want it and away from what they're actually up to.

I've already gone into depth on Planes because it's more complicated than the other methods, so we'll skip that.

Subway

Subways show up in the movies a lot, and honestly they're not far from the truth. There are tons of names for the subway: The Tube. Le Metro. MTR. Metro seems to be the most common name that you'll see, just in different languages or city names. Each city has its own vibe when it comes to their intercity transportation depending on the climate, size of the city, the amount of funding they allocate to the upkeep, etc. Some metro's have a bad rep (sometimes rightfully so) for being unsafe or unreliable while others are safer and smell a lot better. You just never really know what you're going to get.

Here are some good practices as you get used to them. Look up some maps beforehand so it won't be as shocking when you first get there, especially if there's tons of people all pushing around you. I usually take a picture or screenshot of the metro map of the first one I come across so I can map out what I'm looking for or just get a general idea of where everything is at.

You usually have to go down a flight or two of stairs or escalators. There's always some sort of station to buy tickets that look like ATMs on the wall and there's usually some sort of cubby where a person is working during normal business hours. There usually isn't a person stationed at the smaller stops or after a certain time in the evenings, depending on the city.

Most metros use colored lines to designate the routes that certain trains follow. Sometimes they are called numbers or letters or colors, like the A line or Blue line, or Line 4.

Google Maps might be helpful in planning your route if you put where you are and where you're trying to go and then click the little train or bus icon at the top left. There's a good chance that it can tell you what connections you'll need to take and the estimated time those subways are set to arrive or depart.

To buy your metro tickets:
When you go to the ticket machines, tap the screen or a button. There are typically language options to choose from and they often display flags with the name of the language as a guide.

The goal is to look for the destination you're trying to get to or get an adequate amount of money or trips put onto your ticket/card.

Some cities go by destination. This is more typical for metros that go in a straight line. Most cities are bigger than that so they're likely to be more complex.

Some cities go by zones, where it's a flat rate to go anywhere within the designated zone (it should be pretty clearly marked) and they should list what's within that zone. You might have to click in and out of zones to verify what you're looking for.

Some cities go by trips, where you basically buy the number of times you plan to use the card within the standard city limit/zone.

Don't stress out if you get confused, it can be tough to figure out! You can always cancel the transaction or exit and start over if you go too deep into a section that you don't feel is what you're looking for. If you feel like you're holding people up: cancel out, let them go, get back in line and try to follow what locals do as they buy tickets. Just don't creep too hard, lol.

Be sure to look for ways to scroll or arrows on the screen if you feel like your destination isn't being listed, there might be more screens you haven't gotten to yet.

If you're buying "trips" to put on your metrocard, just try to be realistic with how often you plan to use it. You can always add more, but if you overload it and don't use them, it's just wasted.

This one (Berlin) has the zone (the squarish zone) as one flat rate and extra for other lines outside that zone if I remember correctly.

Paying for your metro/ subway ticket:
You can usually pay with cash or card, sometimes it's a good chance to use up some coins you may have and feel like a local. Be sure to smooth out any bills you're trying to use and look at the way they have the bill facing. These machines can be stubborn like that finicky vending machine at work, except the stakes are higher than that tiny bag of Cheetos.

Once it accepts your money, it'll process for a second or lots of seconds until it spits out a ticket. Usually they're below the screen by your knees in a space with a clear lid that you have to push and reach in to grab, probably to make it hard for them to blow away or someone to run by and steal them.

Be sure to stay until it poops out all the tickets that you're expecting (like for the return trip if you bought one) or until the screen defaults back to the start screen. That's always a good indication that the machine is finished with you. It sometimes gives you a receipt automatically too.

Grab and go!

Getting to the trains themselves:
Once you've got the goods, go through the stalls/corrals/turnstiles. This itself can be tricky, trust me. Look ahead of you and see what others are doing. Some cities have just the silver bars that you have to push and walk through. Some have a place to shove in your ticket, it'll turn green and open the doors for you and then you grab your ticket on the other end. Some you just have to scan the ticket on the little screen and wait for it to turn green and open the doors for you.

The important thing is to ALWAYS keep your ticket, never discard it or misplace it in your belongings because you might have to scan it to get out of the station or there might be security that walks around asking to see your ticket to verify you bought one. If it's a short ride, I'd recommend just holding onto it in your hand, putting it in an easy grab place in your wallet or purse, the back of your phone case, or a designated pocket. Just DO NOT lose it.

Getting to the right train:
The walls should have signs displaying which lines are down which tunnels. They usually use the destination at the end of the line as the display name. It's a lot like how highway signs will list the major cities that are in that direction but not every little town along the way. So when you find your destination and the line you need to be on, you might need to look at the last name on that line and follow the signs for that.

You might not get to the right place the first try, so just be patient with yourself, it can feel like a maze sometimes. Luckily this isn't Harry Potter and it won't keep shifting on you with magical creatures and spells. It's just some tunnels and signs that you can TOTALLY figure out. Keep looking at the maps along the way to make sure everything matches up.

Each line goes in two directions (there and back) so you need to be sure you end up on the right side of the tunnel. One side will get on the train going in one direction, the landing on the other side of the tunnel will get on the train going in the opposite direction. You can tell which side by looking at the end destinations listed on that side. If you think you're on the wrong side, just walk back up and look at the tunnels again for the way to cross over.

Once you're in the right place, there's usually a clock there, if you're lucky it says he next expected arrival time.

Once the train arrives, the doors will open and the people currently on the train will exit first, then you can hop on. Make sure to leave room by the doors for them to make their way out before you push in.

Sit tight and enjoy the ride. Be mindful of your possessions and surroundings. Don't talk loudly or take up extra space with your bags if people are looking for seats. Be a decent human and you'll be alright!

The scenes in movies where there are musicians playing or entertainers of other kinds in or on the subway/metro are definitely accurate. That's fairly common and there can be some really talented individuals, just don't let anyone bully you into tipping. DOn't accept anything from anyone, even for free, because they'll likely demand that you pay for it while making a big scene.

Knowing when to get off:
Hopefully you have a general idea of where you're going and the connections you need to catch, but that never stops me from being SO nervous that I'm going to miss my stop or get off too soon. It's the main anxiety that still gets me flustered to this day.

Luckily most trains have the upcoming stops listed on some sort of screen at the front and back of the train car as well as announcing over the comms which stop you're approaching. There's usually a map of some kind listed somewhere on the walls or posters on the train car itself. There's also the name of the stations listed on the walls or roofs of the waiting areas outside the train, they might even have the name of the next stop with an arrow.

Google Maps also has stops in their maps so you might be able to track your progress that way too if you have service. Tunnels might not allow enough service for that at all or might cause a hefty delay on your little blue dot.

A lot of the time, stops that have a major landmark to spot will make reference to it in the name of the stop, like stadiums, major tourist destinations, or airports, etc. That's not always the case though so don't bank on it without checking the maps.

Have your ticket still? I hope so! As you exit the train, look for the exit signs or the little green man light that looks like he's running, that's the way towards the exit commonly used in Europe. You might have to scan or put in your ticket again to exit, then you'll head back up the stairs to the outside world!

You can do it! (:

Trains

Trains are awesome. They're usually pretty smooth rides, fast, fairly comfortable (at least more so than planes), and can often be an affordable method of transportation, especially for long distances by land.

Trains are easy to book. There are a few big providers that go long distances and then more local options that spread out to smaller cities and towns. Some big ones are Amtrak in the US and Eurail in Europe. There's also the Eurostar high-speed train that goes under the English Channel between Paris and London. There are other big names in other areas in the world, just look up the destinations you want to travel between to find your options.

If you're not a regular traveler by train, I think it's pretty easy to forget that it's an option. Like all forms of transportation, the options vary from hella ritsy to super cheap, depending on what you're willing to pay for.

There are so many options so let's go over some factors to think about when you're looking and booking:

Overnight train rides
If you're trying to save some money, look at overnight trains to save on accommodation costs. Some trains have sleeper cars that might be worth it, or you can just try to get the best sleep that you can in the seat. Plus you won't have to waste a day traveling and can get those miles covered while you're asleep to wake up in the new place ready to go!
Some trains have meal cars, showers, and bedrooms available, look into those options!

Passes
There are a lot of options for passes you can get instead of getting individual tickets. There are usually a variety to choose from like unlimited rides in 3 days, 10 days, 30 days or 10 rides to use within 30 days, etc. Explore those packages but take a good, hard look at how often you'd actually use the pass vs what individual ticket prices would look like. Don't assume that you're getting a good deal. Do some quick math to find out. (ticket prices for the trips you plan on taking totaled up vs the pass costs with taxes)

Look for sales! I see sales on those passes all the time, so start looking ahead to see if there are deals. Look around Black Friday or early spring, especially.

Motion sickness
So you know how trains are on a track and they go back and forth on that track? Some trains change the seat direction to face towards the direction the train will be physically going (to or from). I loooove this because I will get crazy motion sickness if I feel like I'm going 90 miles per hour backward. You might be wondering what I mean by how some trains actually change the direction of the seats. Some trains let you pull a lever and the backrest part of the seat will adjust from one end of the seat to the other, allowing you to "change direction" and other trains automatically do it on their own. IT'S AWESOME. Here's a video to show you what I mean in Japan. There are some more futuristic examples I've seen in person, but I didn't record and can't find videos easily online. Just trust me, it's so cool.

Storytime
My first time to Europe I traveled to Spain when I was 18 with my new best friend and main travel partner in crime. Everything was so new to us and it's hilarious to look back now and remember how naive and unprepared we were for that trip. We overpacked, knew barely any Spanish, and barely had any of our traveling skills honed yet. There were quite a few bumps on that trip but one that I find the funniest was when we were trying to get off the train on our return to the airport to go home.

We were sitting with our luggage and once the Aeroporto stop approached, we stood up to get off with our overpacked luggage but the doors never opened! I panicked because the doors had opened for me all the other times we got off the train, but that's because the other passengers knew to hit the button to open the doors. So we were stuck on the train until the next stop. We got off there and had to beg a custodian to let us through to the tunnel that let us get on the train going back to the Airport stop. All in very bad English/Spanish panicked tones at like 6:30 am, mind you. He did take pity on us and we made it to the airport, but it's funny to me now because all I had to do was press stupid the button.

It's important to note that not all trains or subways have a button to press to make the doors open, some have levers, and most open automatically, but it's just fun to me to look back at the silly little mistakes I've made along the way. Remember, we all start somewhere. I'm nowhere near done making mistakes, but I know I'll be able to laugh them off later.

Buses

There's not a ton to add about busses because most of the same rules apply to trains. There are stations to get on similar to trains although most are just pavilions without much indoor space other than the offices and a bathroom usually (but not always).

Some busses are stinky and dingy with spotty AC and strange people, but others are super clean with TVs on the back of the seats with great AC and nice people. You just don't always know what you're going to get!

They are usually cheaper options though, so they're worth checking out. Overnight bus rides are fairly common if you're on a budget, but they do not provide a great night's sleep. Up to you and your budget.

Boats / Ferry

Boats probably won't be a common form of transport unless you're island hopping, but with places like Greece and Croatia to see, it's worth mentioning.

Boats and Ferry tickets work very similarly to buses and trains, google what you're looking to do and your options will pop up. I'd recommend showing up early to the port or dock to get better seats (or seats at all) as they are usually first come first serve. You might want to be on the side with the prettier view, remember to think of things in terms of the direction the boat will be going, not the orientation of the boat at the dock.

In my experience, docks and ports are not very clearly marked and lack general signs, **so again, get there early!** It can take a lot longer than you anticipated to get to the right area and find the right boat. Don't hesitate to ask people questions, they might be grumpy about it, but it's better than being lost and missing your chance to board.

Cars

Depending on the trip you're taking, you might need to get a ride somewhere or rent a car.

Renting a car

I typically use Enterprise but go with whatever has the best deal. Here are the notes that I have on renting a car.

- If you're under 25, there will likely be a young driver's fee or restriction.
- You should probably get some form of insurance, the level of how much coverage is up to you and where you're driving.
- Always be sure to specify if you need automatic or if you can drive manual (stick).
- You have to return the car with the same level of gas that you left with or they'll charge you for it, probably at a higher rate than gas prices are.
- Pack your USB cord to plug into the car. It'll charge your phone and Bluetooth can be spotty sometimes.
- Take the time to familiarize yourself with where different things are (windshield wipers, blinkers, climate controls, GPS, etc) so you're not doing it on the road while driving.
- There are often deals when booking a car rental if you have AAA or a program through an employer, be sure to check them out!
- When you get to the car rental location, have your ID, insurance card, and payment ready to go so check-in goes smoother.
- Be sure to ask about returning after hours or how to get back into the lot if it's fenced in.
- Renting a car from the airport is usually more expensive, but that's no big deal if it's your only option. But if you can, look at nearby locations before booking.

That's the basics that I've learned over the years. There are tons more resources online!

Uber and Lyft

Most people know how Uber and Lyft work nowadays. To summarize the process: you download the app, put in a payment method, input where you are and where you'd like to go, request a driver, a driver accepts the job, driver comes to pick you up, and they take you to your destination. The payment is charged to your card and you are able to review the driver and they're able to review you as a passenger.

It works the same abroad too! Some cities have different rules, some cities just use one platform more than the other, etc.

I usually do a quick check on the app, I'll put in some generic location like an airport like I'm booking a ride somewhere to see how many little cars show up. It's also helpful to get an idea of how much it would cost to get from the airport to your accommodation or downtown as you price things out.

Sometimes language barriers can be difficult when you have a hard time finding each other in busy locations, but it's still pretty seamless wherever I go.

Blablacar

Blablacar is a carpooling service. It's similar to Uber and Lyft, except these drivers are on their own trips and they're willing to bring passengers along to get them closer to their destinations. You just share the cost of the trip, agreeing on terms before the trip. I know people who have used it and had pleasant experiences, plus there were over 70 million users in 2019 in over 22 countries. So it's pretty vetted. Consider looking into it if it seems like a good fit for you! The link I have is for the France site, but just google Blablacar and the country you want to use it in.

Countries: Belgium, Brazil, Croatia, Czech Republic, France, Germany, Hungary, India, Italy, Luxembourg, Mexico, The Netherlands, Poland, Portugal, Romania, Russia, Serbia, Slovakia, Spain, Turkey, Ukraine, and the United Kingdom.

Vans

I gotta tell ya, I love a great van road trip. I've been on two big trips this way and they are such a blast. There's nothing else like freedom on the road. So, if you don't have a driver's license, I'm sorry! Skip ahead.

Van trips are not for everyone, but they are great if you want to see a lot of places in the wilderness that don't have a lot of other ways of getting there. If you're yearning to reconnect with nature, I'd highly recommend van life. It keeps you sheltered from the elements, extremely mobile and it offers you the freedom to go at your own pace and endless opportunities.

Most people take longer trips in a converted van. A conversion van is a cargo van that is outfitted with various luxuries for road trips and camping. Converted means that the van is tweaked or renovated to include other features, for example, a bed, table, sink, storage, etc. Some are super fancy with all the works and others are pretty basic but practical.

Here's the interior of the Escape Campervan that I rented in the Pacific Northwest with my bestie.

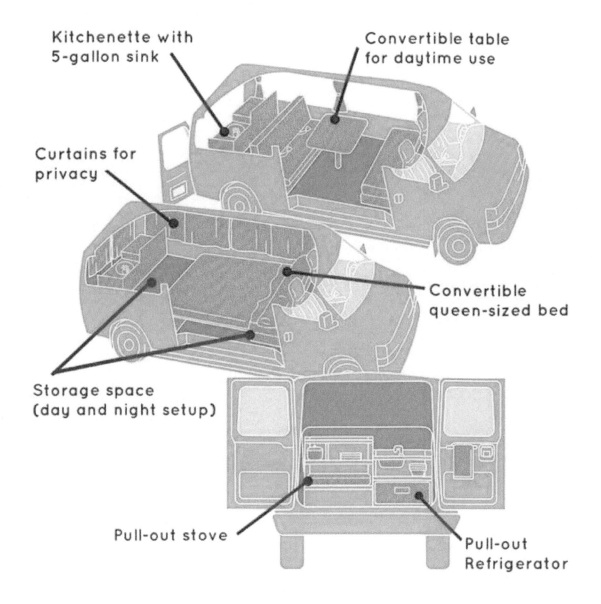

Kitchenette with 5-gallon sink

Convertible table for daytime use

Curtains for privacy

Convertible queen-sized bed

Storage space (day and night setup)

Pull-out stove

Pull-out Refrigerator

I've never converted a van myself (but my awesome parents are!) so I can only really speak to renting vans that are already converted. There were tons of options to choose from in Iceland which was awesome! They still recommend that you stay in campgrounds to protect the natural beauty and environment but I'll be honest, we mostly boondocked where we could on the side of the road around the entire island.

In the US, there are much, much fewer options, most are in the Pacific Northwest, California, Colorado, and Utah. There's a lot of rules involved and it can be tricky if you're not doing a round trip to return the van to the location that you booked it from. The good news is that if you're traveling with other people, it makes this type of trip so much more affordable since you can split most of the costs like gas rental, cleaning, insurance, and the extra miles fees.

Redwood National Forest, California

Things that I learned from van research:
- Most van rental companies in the US want drivers to be 25 and only a few let 21-24-year-olds rent them. Other countries are more lenient with 18+ with proof of a driver's license from your home country.
- Your domestic driver's license is sufficient, it must be valid (not expired).
- If you have car insurance, it covers you as a driver which is a good start but I'd still recommend getting the van insurance to cover other possibilities that aren't covered by your insurance, you'll have to research that coverage specifically. Plan to add that cost to your budget.
- Beware of the mileage per day policy. Most of the time you get an allotted mileage and then you're charged a rate for the miles that you drive past that number. It's usually much less than a dollar per mile, but depending on how far you're going, that can add up.
- Most vans are easier to drive than you think, but try to practice parallel parking in your car so you can get comfortable before possibly having to do it in a big van.
- Don't forget to put the gas cap back on after filling up (oops).

- Be prepared with various methods of driving entertainment. Don't plan to talk 100% of the time; you or your travel partner will likely go insane. Playlists, podcasts, and audiobooks can all be downloaded and are a blessing.

If you're a planner like me, we had great success with using Google My Maps. It lets you open a map and pinpoint spots of interest, name and categorize them, and work on it with your travel partner in real-time. We used it as just general points to look at as options as we drove along the Pacific North Coast through Washington, Oregon, and a bit of California.

It made it really easy to familiarize ourselves with the options that we'd be driving by and a great tool to look at what we'd want to visit that day. The links to the Google page were super helpful and I downloaded it so we had it available even when we didn't have service.

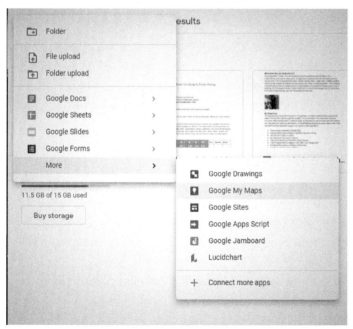

I'm sure there are other tools, but I loved using this free one.

We colored each state in one color, took advantage of the icons you can assign, and put little comments in while we were researching so we could keep things straight as we filtered through sooo many options.

Google Timeline
Also, a creepy but possibly fun fact that you can see where you've been traveling through your Google Timeline via your location is turned on your phone. You'll have to sort through your settings to turn this off.

This is where I have been throughout North America between 2018-2021. Pretty crazy, but it's not entirely accurate. I was also in Las Vegas, so take it with a grain of salt.

Here are some general packing tips for van life that I loved:
(you can find tons more in the countless articles out there to best fit your type of trip)

- Pack quarters for showers! It's usually around a quarter for a minute or so. Plan accordingly.
- Bring a deck of cards
- Definitely bring headlamps. You can put them over the headrest of the front seats to light up the inside of the van well.
- We loved using bins. We had a dishes bin, bathroom stuff bin, and general supplies bin that made it easy to clear out the back of the van at night by putting the bins in the front seats and returning them in the morning.
- Buy or bring fast drying water shoes. You don't want a wet foot stank in the van.
- Have a "rag" towel for dusting off your equipment or shoes or body
- Get cups that fit in the cup holders that have lids with straws! It's' a hassle to have to open water bottles, take lids off, etc while driving a big van. Have your bigger water bottles for exploring too.
- Lawn chairs are great to have!
- Having a smaller bag to take your clothes with you to the shower and be able to hang up is super handy. Most spots to put things down can get wet or be yucky.
- Bring wet wipes. Trust me. Some toilet paper is a good idea too.
- Download movies if you need an escape on a tough day or if you're waiting out the rain.

Remember Shalee from Shalee Wanders?

Here's her advice about Van Life and road-tripping

"It's been over four years since we renovated a rusted GMC Savannah and took it across the country for six months. In the beginning, we spent more time in repair shops than on the road. The beginning was filled with harsh realities and a constant hum of uncertainty. Running on low bank accounts and a thirst for adventure, we didn't have much, and maybe that ended up being the best part.

With Van Life or long road trips in general, it sounds like a pipe dream. We often see the edited photos and videos of people living their "best life" in the world's most beautiful locations. Making dinner on the Pacific Coast as the waves perfectly crash against the cluster of reflecting rocks at low tide. Waking up to cotton candy sunrises with an expansive and unobstructed view of the cloudless Mount Rainier. You can picture the exact images I'm describing.

Don't get me wrong, it is every bit that magical. It's also pretty tough.

There are three rules to follow when planning an extensive road trip

1. Never make an itinerary
2. Embrace the road bumps
3. Ditch Instagram's most "sought after" locations

Never Make an Itinerary

The freedom comes in the lack of schedule. Allow yourself to completely let go. As someone who often needed (and still sometimes does) complete control of a situation, it can be fearful and anxiety-ridden to completely let go. You can thank me later. I will never feel that free again.

Embrace the Road Bumps

Road tripping is hard. Really hard. Especially if traveling with a significant other or friend, it is going to be emotionally and physically taxing. There is nowhere to hide when living out of a van together. If you're not in your tiny makeshift home, you're exposed to the elements. Your car with having flashing headlights that allow you to hit three repair shops in less than 60 miles. You'll be trapped sleeping in a carpark under a San Francisco bridge for three nights due to flooding on your route north. You'll definitely get kicked out of several attempted camp locations in Southern California. It's bound to happen. Get pissed, release a tear, laugh a little, then tie up your travelin' shoes and hit the road again.

Ditch Instagram's Top Location

Real talk: many of my most disappointing adventures have been to location clogging every wanderlust Instagram feed. A lot of places have been discovered. More haven't. Instead of copying what has been done, discover something new. You'd be surprised what's at the end of a long dirt road you decided to take in remote Southern Utah."   Thanks, Shalee!

Some of my Van Life Pictures

Iceland

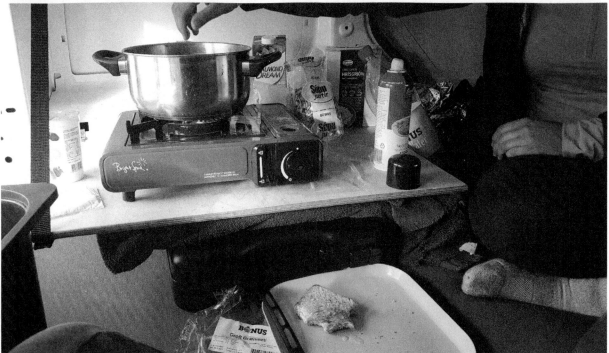

Key Takeaways for Transportation

- Practice great caution of your belongings in transportation hubs, it's pickpocket paradise.
- There are tons of ways to get around, but some are better than others depending on where you're traveling to. Search around for your best options.
- Buses and trains are super helpful getting around especially in Europe and other areas with major cities, but cars and vans are often more available in the US.
- Do a little digging when planning to depend on rideshare options. They may not always be available. You might need to try both Lyft and Uber.

FINANCING

Alright folks, let's talk about money. Traveling is not cheap so one thing I hear aaaalll the time is "I wish I had the money to travel but…(insert excuse here)"

Let's agree on one thing right here, right now. If you're going to read this chapter, you're agreeing to the terms and conditions that you are no longer accepting excuses for why you don't have the money and are looking for ways to round up the money to make this happen. If not, then go scroll through Instagram and find your motivation to commit to making your dream trip a reality. *Clicks "I am not a robot" to proceed*

Tips on Saving Money.
I have a lot of little tips I've used over the years to develop the habit of saving rather than spending. Keyword there is *habit*. You can't expect to save a boatload of money overnight, it takes sometimes a few years depending on your circumstances. Let's get the obvious ones out of the way.

- Cut out unnecessary expenses right off the bat (mindless shopping, frequent Starbucks, sales items because they're on sale)

- Find ways to share expenses (Netflix, Prime, bulk toilet paper)

- Buy second hand. Scour Facebook Marketplace or buy, sell, trade pages in your neighborhood. You'd be surprised at the nice stuff you can find within 20 miles of you.

- Sell items you don't actually need. Take on the great purge! Ask your family if they have anything they want to donate to your cause to sell for some money. You'd be surprised what people are looking for on Facebook Marketplace.

- Limit eating out. I know this tip is everywhere, but it's insane how much it adds up. Especially drinks, ever heard of pre-gaming and Uber?

- Analyze your spending habits. Sometimes all you need is a nice pie chart that shows what categories you're putting your money to. Some banks like Chase have a strong algorithm that already makes good guesses at what category certain expenses fall into (Energy bill = utility, gas station = car expense, restaurant = Dining out) taking the majority of the work off your shoulders. Do yourself a favor and be sure not to take a drink of anything when you finally see the report. #SpitTake #WetLaptop

- Find free money. Are you in college or university? APPLY FOR ANY AND ALL SCHOLARSHIPS. Yeah, no one wants to spend 2 hours after they've been working or doing other school work writing scholarship essays, but let's put things into perspective. Let's say there's a $5,000 scholarship and you meet all the requirements. If you make $13 an hour, it would take over 385 hours of labor to make that kind of money in a world where you didn't even have to pay taxes. Two hours doesn't sound so bad now does it? Besides, you know all the answers because it's most likely asking questions about you! The less you have to pay for tuition, the more you can add to the travel fund. Cha-ching!

College tip: Make a Google doc and save all your responses to scholarship applications there. Chances are you'll be able to pull from what you already wrote for other applications. Add to it every year, no one will remember what you wrote last year, so make it easier on yourself.

Research grants- Also for those of you in school, look for opportunities through the usual options like independent studies, travel abroad programs and scholarships, etc. What you might not have thought about are research grants. I was lucky enough to go to a school that had money set aside for undergrad research projects and funds to cover travel expenses. Here's how that worked: I was working on a paper with one of my professors for their research requirements (professors usually have to write so many papers/do research and get so many of them published if they want tenure or raises).

So, he brings up the idea of me presenting our paper at a business research conference at OXFORD UNIVERSITY. Terrifying, right? So as pale-faced and nervous as I was, I agreed that it'd be awesome and we submitted the paper to the conference. You wait a while to get an email back telling you if your paper was accepted or not. Ours was accepted 2 weeks later! So I'm hit with the reality of how am I going to A) not pass out and B) get myself to England for that conference. So Mr. Prof helps me fill out the undergrad research grant paperwork which covered: the conference fee (Anywhere between $100-$600, depending on the size of the conference), overnight accommodations, transportation expenses, and related travel expenses (parking costs, train tickets, etc.)

It may work differently at different schools but mine was a tiered allowance: up to $600 regional, $1,000 national, and $1,500 international conferences. I did have to pay for everything out of pocket and submit all my receipts for everything related to the conference, but they reimbursed me a week and a half later. I got a week in England, Scotland, and France 85% covered because of that grant. All I had to do was write a paper with a professor, make a presentation and present it at a conference. Public speaking might not be everyone's favorite activity, but when I look back now, that conference was just 6 hours out of my week of fun with my mom. She was a trooper and kept up with me, backpacking it across 5 major cities (Paris, London, Oxford, Edinburgh, Glasgow).

Storytime:

I loved this process so much that I talked that professor into being my professor for an independent study where the main objective was to write another paper (I chose the topic of sustainability), get it accepted into another conference, and present it. This time the chosen conference was in Dubrovnik, Croatia.

The best part of it all, I got my best friend to join me in this project so we could both go! Since I already used the travel grant, I couldn't do it again, but she could. So we went through the same project as before, but it was awesome because not only did it pay for a huge chunk for her trip, it covered a lot of my expenses too since we shared the overnight accommodations and transportation methods. I did have to buy my plane tickets, but Uber/Lyft was all covered. Sneaky, right? There's free money out there if you ask the right questions. The best part of that whole trip was that the conference included a full-day boat tour to 3 islands with lunch and drinks, we had an absolute blast with those Ph.D. students and professors from all over the world that day.

Research grants might not be an option for you, but if there's any chance that it is - look into it, pal.

Travel Credit Cards
Okay, I want to take some time here to explain how I view and use credit cards. It's too important and misunderstood to be noted in bullet points. Disclaimer here: I'm no financial expert and in no way telling you how to live your life, but I'm going to dump my opinions here anyways. Feel free to skip right past this part down to the mind tricks.
For everyone who wants a lil financial lesson, Let's go.

Credit cards can be easily abused or extremely helpful, depending on your spending habits. Here's a simple rule to follow that will never steer you wrong. **Don't spend money that you don't have**. It's that simple. Credit cards can seem like a "get out of jail free" card, and sometimes they can really help you in a pinch, but I'm a firm believer in never carrying over a balance(spending money I don't have), therefore never paying interest. I use my credit card like a debit card, if I don't have the money in my account to cover it, I don't buy it, and I autopay the full balance every single month. I've had credit cards since my 18th birthday and I've never paid a cent in interest. Some people believe in getting cards that give you a year with no interest to give them time to buy something and pay it off in time, and that's fine, just be careful. That's a dangerous cycle to get trapped in.

I absolutely do not recommend that you get a travel credit card to put the whole trip on that you can't afford and say "C'est la vie, I'll worry about it after the fact" without being able to afford it. But here's a list of how a travel credit card can really help you in the long run.

- Builds a healthy credit history and credit score (good for when you take out loans, apply for apartments, try to get a mortgage, etc)
- Helps practice self-control and financial stability
- Promotional packages allow for spending perks (if you spend $X amount by X days, you get $X in rewards)
- Cashback options or other point gain (2 points on all travel expenses, 1 point for every dollar spent kind of things) can turn into lots of goodies like points→ cashback, discounts on travel bookings, or gift cards. Can your debit card do that? Probably not.
- Some credit cards have travel insurance included on purchases made on that card
- Most have no international transaction fees
- Visa and Mastercard are accepted all around the world
- Big-name banks all have 24/7 helplines, your hometown bank probably won't be able to help.
- If used separately, travel credit cards keep all travel expenses together and separate from your other stuff

Credit cards may not be right for you, and that's totally fine. It's worth looking into if there is a card out there that might fit your needs. I get hundreds of dollars worth of rewards and I'm a pretty modest spender if I do say so myself. I'm just suggesting you research and make your own educated decision.

MIND TRICKS

Let's talk about some mind tricks that I play on myself to help. Can I see right through them because I placed them on myself? DUH. But it helps to kickstart your brain into a different view of what you need to spend and what money can be for traveling if you let it be. Remember, you're the reason you haven't traveled yet. No one is making you spend your money. No one is forcing you to have Spotify Premium or a new iPhone. No one is forcing you to love take-out food. Take responsibility for the life you want to live and the memories you want to make.

- <u>Do I want this here or there?</u> This is a game I would play every time I wanted a little treat or to go out to eat or see something I didn't need at the grocery store. Here's how it works: I would ask myself "Do I want this half gallon of Cookie Dough ice cream to eat alone in my bedroom or do I want to buy gelato from the cute guy on the Italian cobblestone streets?" No brainer there, so I'd walk away.

- <u>High five</u> This one is simple. For a while, any five dollar bill I came in contact with I put in my travel fund box. It added up a lot for me since I was getting cash tips at the time. Today wouldn't be as effective since I hardly handle cash anymore. Make up your own rule. #creditcard

- <u>Hide and Seek</u> This one may not work for everyone or every lifestyle, but it is effective for my brain. I would take cash out of my account and put it into my travel fund so it would be deducted from my Account Balance. Since it wasn't in my account, it was like I couldn't spend it. To further the hiding part, I kept that box waaaay under my bed, so it was too much of a chore to get the box out and be tempted to pull any money from it and I wanted to put a good chunk of cash in it every time I got it out.

HOW MUCH TO SAVE

So the next big question is: "How much should I save?" That will always be variable depending on all the questions above, even down to what weekend you try to go. Holiday prices can skyrocket the costs of flights and accommodations, so do your research. There's no magical number. There's waaaay too much fluctuation in prices for me to even try to set a dollar range for you. Different countries, cities, activities range from cheap to hella expensive. You'll need to tweak this to match what's more important to you, that's part of what this book is all about, after all.

WHAT YOU SPEND MONEY ON IS ENTIRELY UP TO YOU.
THE COST OF YOUR TRIP IS BASED ENTIRELY OFF OF YOUR CHOICES.
Spend wisely, my friends.

The best way I can do this is to set percentages that are GUIDELINES. I cannot express enough how this is not the best, perfect or only way to budget. I'm just trying to give you an idea of what to expect. Let's say that your trip is over and you have to tally up all your expenses and you get the total cost of the trip. That total = 100%. This might be how it broke down for one week in one country, traveling to different cities but staying within the country lines. (Traveling between countries is typically more expensive than within one country)

I hope you get great flight prices, but you should plan for them to be a huge portion of the trip cost.
DISCLAIMER: ONLY ROUGH GUIDELINES! There's no one size fits all.

Flights		30%
Transportation		10%
Meals	Breakfast	3%
	Lunch	3%
	Dinner	5%
Treats / Drinks		4%
Activities		20%

Accommodations		25%
	TOTAL	100%

How much to budget for

Like the layout of this book describes, I think you should narrow down what you ABSOLUTELY are thrilled about doing, find out that cost, and make other decisions around those activities in your preliminary research (aka find cheaper places to sleep). If what you would love to do is sail on a huge yacht for a month around the Mediterranean, then a) me too! and b) get real honey, you wouldn't be reading this book if that was in your budget. If you're being realistic, then you should be able to intuitively know what's within reason or not when it comes to your budget.

I'll give some rough estimates for what a few different kinds of trips have cost so you have an idea.

A week in Costa Del Sol, Spain's southern coast	Split accommodation cost with a friend, stayed in the same city with day trips to 3 other cities (Flights from Toronto, Canada to Malaga, Spain)	Flight = $550 Hotel = $225 (my portion) Food = $200 Fun = $120 **TOTAL =** **$1,095**
10 days Europe Tour on a tight budget, 5 countries	Split some accommodation, mostly stayed in hostels and only ate 2 meals a day. Slept on overnight bus rides twice	Somewhere around $2,500 Scored a $17 flight from Brussels to Dublin on Ryanair **$2,500**
7 days in Croatia	Split all accommodations but traveled to multiple cities and islands. Island hopping trip was paid for by the conference we attended to present paper. #freefun	Flight = $950 (kinda standard) AirBnbs = $260 (my portion) Food = $220 Fun = $250 **TOTAL =** **$1,680**
Month-long trip with a week in Southern Europe and the rest in Southeast Asia	Took about 14 flights total throughout several cities in Portugal, Spain, Thailand, Malaysia, and Japan. Accommodations split in SE Asia	Somewhere around $4,000 **$4,000**
7 days in an all-inclusive resort in the Dominican Republic	Flights from Detroit, MI, all-inclusive adults resort, full-day excursion, resort split two ways	Flight = $400 Resort = $1,600 (my portion) Fun = $200 **TOTAL =** **$ 2,200**
5 days in Puerto Rico	Splitting accommodations and	Flight = $400

	transportation (ubers and car rental)	AirBnbs = $200(my portion) Food = $180 Fun = $300 **TOTAL =** **$1,080**
Domestic weekend getaway	4 days in Austin, Texas Splitting accommodations and transportation (ubers)	Flights = $220 AirBnb = $175 Food = $125 Fun = $275 **TOTAL =** **$795**

I've said it before and I'll say it again, what the cost of your trip comes out to is ENTIRELY on you and the choices that you make. Being prepared can often help lower that cost, but at the end of the day, every choice you make has a cost. The drink, meals, more convenient ways of transportation, fancier or cute places to stay all add up to your trip cost, so really think about how much you have available to spend and what you're choosing to spend it on.

PREPARING

You've got the trip planned and you're ready to go. Here are some things to take care of before you go.

LEARNING THE LANGUAGE

This one probably comes to mind for a lot of us. Not sure about you, but it's always been so daunting for me. The idea of having to learn a language, speak it, AND have to try to understand when people speak it to me sends my anxiety through the roof. But, that's how I know it's a good opportunity to push myself to grow.

Here's what I believe:

1. You should always at least try to learn the basics. Hello, goodbye, thanks, please, yes, no, excuse me, and how much are my go tos. You would be surprised how far those few words will get you and how much body language and visual cues in the world can fill in the rest to get a minimum understanding of the situation even if you don't know a single word other than that list. Duolingo is an app that is a fun way to get the basics down.

2. Learning more is fantastic, of course, but you can't let language become an obstacle from going. Yes, it's terrifying to go to countries that don't even use the same alphabet as you, and you'll struggle sometimes, but have faith, okay? For my fellow English speakers, I still can't express how fortunate we are to have our primary or only language be so widely used. On some level, we'll forever and always take that for granted, but it is a huge advantage that we should recognize, appreciate, and capitalize on. So my main

belief here is that there are only benefits to learning as much of the language as you can, but even if you don't, you'll be able to manage somehow.

3. <u>Technology is your language best friend. Use it.</u> Google translate will never be perfect (language is so complicated and continuously evolving), but dang is it getting better all the time. One of the apps to download (you'll see the list coming up soon later in the book) is Google Translate. There are options to download specific languages so you can look up stuff in offline mode when you don't have data or wifi. I always try to do this, but honestly, I didn't use it as much as I originally thought. It is a great resource to have available though and can get you out of a pickle when you need it.

4. <u>If you don't use it, you'll lose it.</u> Ask any person that's studied language and they'll tell you that it's unbelievably true that if you don't speak the language every once in a while, you'll likely get rusty. If you don't use your language skills for years, you could forget a substantial amount. It should come back to you pretty quickly though once you start to use it again, don't worry.

GETTING A PASSPORT

You're going abroad! Time to get a US Passport book.

The whole process is relatively easy but there is paperwork and prep work. Overall the prep work prior to submitting everything could be in a couple of days, butonce it's submitted, you could have it in your hands in anywhere between 4-12 weeks. Travel.gov says routine times are 10-12 weeks and expedited are 4-6 weeks, but mine only took 3 weeks. So obviously you should give the process plenty of time before your actual trip (I'm talking like 3 months, minimum.), but there's a chance it'll come fairly quickly. Different times of year take longer as the office has high and low seasons. Think of everyone getting ready for spring break at the last minute.

Quick info sesh on passports. There are 4 kinds of passports, but we general travelers only need to know about the regular passport book. Passports for an American (16+ years old) lasts for 10 years from the issue date and 5 years for minors (under the age of 16). You may renew your passport for a fee once that 10 years is approaching (I recommend renewing it at the 9 years 6-month mark).

<u>Passport Book Forms and Fees</u>
Applying for a passport for the first time will require filling out Form DS-11 and paying a $110 application fee and $35 acceptance fee. Renewing a passport will cost the $110 application fee once again.
Children's passport books cost an $85 application fee and a $35 acceptance fee.

Side note on getting a passport for a child: both parents have to be there in person or have a notarized statement of permission from the other, just a heads up.

Passport Card:

This is a Variation of the Regular Passport that can be used the same as a regular passport, but with certain restrictions. It may only be used for land and sea travel to Bermuda, Canada, the Caribbean, and Mexico and cannot be used for international air travel.

So basically this could be a good option for those who drive through Canada and Mexico.

The Process of Getting a passport book:

So where do you start? Google, duh.

1. Google "passport application" to get Form DS-11 (or click this link) and fill out the form.
2. Gather the following documents
   a. PROOF OF U.S. CITIZENSHIP: Evidence of U.S. citizenship AND a photocopy of the front (and back, if there is printed information) must be submitted with your application. The photocopy must be on 8 ½ inches by 11-inch paper, black and white ink, legible, and clear. Evidence that is not damaged, altered, or forged will be returned to you. Note: Lawful permanent resident cards submitted with this application will be forwarded to U.S. Citizenship and Immigration Services if they determine that you are a U.S. citizen.
   b. PROOF OF IDENTITY: You must present your original identification AND submit a photocopy of the front and back with your passport application.
   c. RECENT COLOR PHOTOGRAPH: Photograph must meet passport requirements – full front view of the face and 2x2 inches in size. (Many Walgreens, post offices, and county buildings offer this service for a fee.)

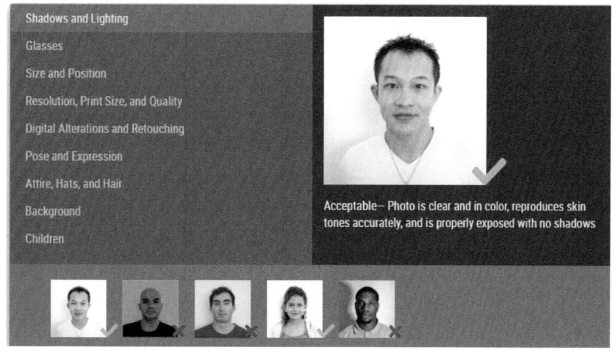

3. Either mail it in or look for a online

4. Pay the fee. visit travel.state.gov for current fees.
5. Wait for your "citizen evidence" to come back and then your passport. They are not typically mailed together (in case the package got lost or stolen both would be gone).
6. You're all set to fly abroad!

NEW Electronic Passport info

Here's the language from the Department of State:

> "The U.S. Department of State now issues an "Electronic Passport" book, which contains an embedded electronic chip. The electronic passport book continues to be proof of the bearer's U.S. citizenship/nationality and identity, and looks and functions in the same way as a passport without a chip.
>
> The addition of an electronic chip in the back cover enables the passport book to carry a duplicate electronic copy of all information from the data page. The electronic passport book is usable at all ports-of-entry, including those that do not yet have electronic chip readers.
>
> Use of the electronic format provides the traveler the additional security protections inherent in chip technology. Moreover, when used at ports-of-entry equipped with electronic chip readers, the electronic passport book provides for faster clearance through some of the port-of-entry processes.
>
> The electronic passport book does not require special handling or treatment, but like previous versions should be protected from extreme heat, bending, and immersion in water. The electronic chip must be read using specially formatted readers, which protects the data on the chip from unauthorized reading.
>
> The cover of the electronic passport book is printed with a special symbol representing the embedded chip. The symbol will appear in port-of-entry areas where the electronic passport book can be read."

Source: DS-11 Form

My takeaway from this: We're in a digital world now. This is nothing to be concerned about, only a step towards efficiency. This is one of those things that are just out of our control.

For domestic flights, the TSA is requiring everyone to upgrade to the Real ID by May 2022 (was 2020 but pushed due to COVID-19).

Be sure to go to your state's government website to see how you can get your ID renewed with the Star. They have FAQ pages.

WHAT TO HAVE PRINTED PHYSICALLY

We're in a digital world, for sure, but some things still need to be on paper. Here are some tips on what you need to look out for.

Some reservations/ tickets NEED to be in printed form to be accepted. There's not a clear rule that "all of these types need to be printed" so I can't give you a list. But, I can let you know that some places that you may make reservations at may say "printed physical ticket is the only accepted form of reservation" or something similar. You NEED to check your confirmation emails for the details on whether or not this is the case. I've booked bus tickets from Paris to Amsterdam that are just the driver with a scanner and if you didn't have the paper with the bar code, he wouldn't let you on the bus. I have similar stories with concert tickets, train and boat tickets, Groupon vouchers, and tours. Luckily more and more is becoming digital, but I don't want you stuck in a pickle because you assumed your confirmation email would be enough. Either print it at home and take it with you (easy) or figure out a way to print it while you're abroad (not so easy).

What to do if you need to print something? If you're staying at a hostel or a hotel, try to ask the front desk if they will print for you. Some have computer stations available (possibility for a fee) or they can tell you a local option. Google is always helpful. DO NOT WAIT TILL THE LAST MINUTE. I can't tell you how unreliable some services can be, the hours listed online don't always mean the store will be open, so give yourself plenty of time and focus on getting it done well inside the window of normal business hours.

Have copies printed of your important documents to have a spare at home. Make sure a trusted person at home knows where they are and how to access them. For me, my mom is my backup person on the ground. She helps me research when I don't have access or makes a call that I couldn't do internationally. I haven't had to ask yet, but she's prepared to send me copies of my passport, license, birth certificate, insurance information, etc whenever I might need them. Don't have someone that you trust with that information? Make digital copies and put them in a secure folder, there are lots of options like emailing them to yourself, having a password-protected folder, etc, figure out what you're most comfortable with. I find it to be useful to have a picture of my passport and insurance info saved that I have access to easily and quickly when I need to book flights or fill out medical forms.

Optional: Depends on what kind of person you are, but if you're an anxious type that always wants to have quick access to what times, dates, and companies you're booked with so you can double-check them, try this. I take screen clippings (Snipping Tool on Windows computers, Shift, Command, and 4 on Macs) and put them all on one page, and then print that out the week of my trip. It gives me peace to have it there in front of me when there's a lot of moving pieces to a trip, especially when I was getting started. It would look something like this:

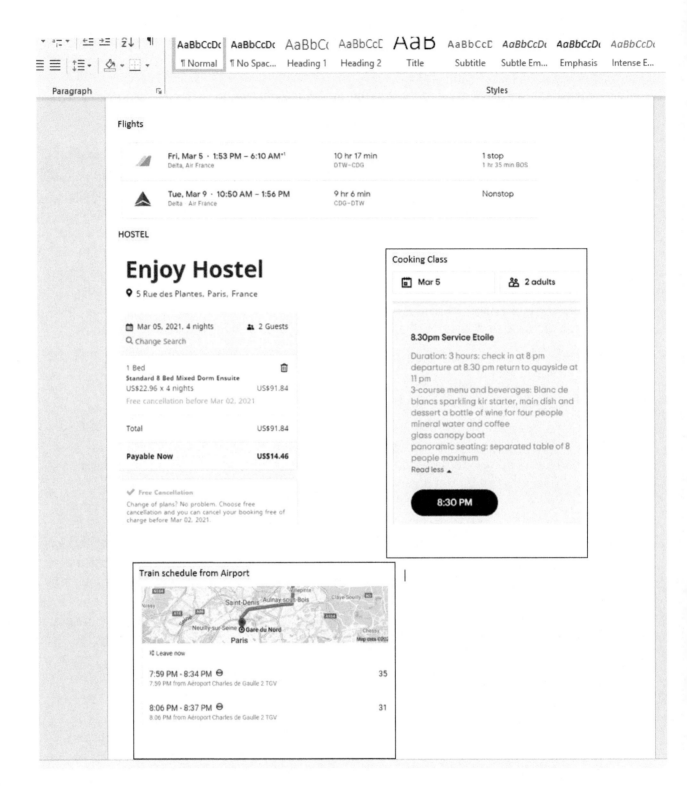

What's safe to eat or drink

This is a must! You need to be aware of where you can and cannot drink water from the tap (even for brushing your teeth, washing your face). You can usually use a Google Search to find out. Some areas within a country may be safe to drink the water from and others may not, use your best judgment and always use caution when you're unsure. The few cents or dollars it takes to buy water at the store is always going to be worth avoiding the pain that may ensue if you catch a bug.

I'm a huge advocate for producing the least amount of waste possible, especially when it comes to single-use plastics like water bottles, but your health and safety trumps the need to be eco-conscious in my opinion. When there are more sustainable options available, by all means, please take them, but don't sacrifice your wellbeing for a few bottles. There are sometimes safe water refill stations or larger containers of water that you can buy to refill your own bottle. Some hotels, hostels, or other accommodations will provide options for safe drinking water, and most hosts post a sign in the bathrooms whether the tap is safe for consumption or not.

As for food, it's much more difficult to know what's safe or not, but there are some guidelines to follow.

Street food can be anything from sketchy to absolutely delicious. It'd be a shame to miss out on some of the best or most iconic foods out of fear of street vendors being unreputable. Here are points to consider:
- Try to get recommendations from a local, they know who are better options
- Look for places where there is a bit of a line
- Try to go places that you can see the food being prepared
- Look for proper cooling or heating chambers being used
- Look for fresh batches being made
- Research well-reviewed vendors
- Use your nose. If it smells different, nbd you're probably not used to the spices or ingredients, but if it smells *off*, avoid it.
- Find streets that have multiple vendors, competition is a good thing from a customer's perspective.

Appropriate dress attire for special sites
We all want to have cute outfits on for our pictures in front of the Eiffel Tower, duh. But some places, usually religious buildings, have a dress code that must be met to be allowed in. A lot of major churches in Italy, for example, have the reputation of not allowing visitors unless their knees and shoulders are covered. The same expectations go for a ton of temples in Asian countries like Thailand and Japan.

While we're on the topic of temples, you're also expected to remove your shoes before entering most temples. This is a sign of respect, remember that these places hold much significance to others and should be treated as such by respecting their rules and following the lead of the locals. There's sometimes a place to put your shoes, but often you just leave them at the front steps out of the way of the walkway.

Let's say you're in a city or destination that is on the sea or ocean. Excluding beachside huts and ice cream carts, most establishments do not want you walking around in your swimwear, whether you have some form of "beachy cover-up" or not. They expect at least some form of day attire and shoes. So put some clothes on.. Light summer dresses are super easy options for women anyways, but especially for situations like these mentioned.

We'll talk more about general clothing packing tips at the end.

Key Takeaways for Preparing:

- Check reservation emails to see if you need physically printed tickets
- Have back up copies/pictures of important documents, digitally and physically
- Know if the activity you're dying to do booked up months/week in advance
- Check which days your must-see activities are open (google it or call ahead)
- Churches often require knees and shoulders to be covered (maybe even ankles)
- Temples expect the same and you have to take your shoes off
- Be prepared with layers when going to religious buildings

Currency

Let's talk about dolla bills.
You're probably going to want cash for some things, but cards will be accepted in most places. Let's just talk about cash for now.

Exchange rates

An exchange rate is basically how much of Currency A will get you in Currency B. Some countries have very high valued currencies (because they're "safer" or more trustworthy) and are worth more than others. Exchange rates are constantly fluctuating and are dependent on more factors than you and I will ever understand. All we need to know is what the current exchange rate is at the time of purchasing the new currency.

You can Google what the current exchange rates are by typing in your currency compared to the currency you're looking to use. For example, "US Dollar to British Pound". This will tell you how much your home currency will be worth in the other currency. You'll get a tool that looks like this:

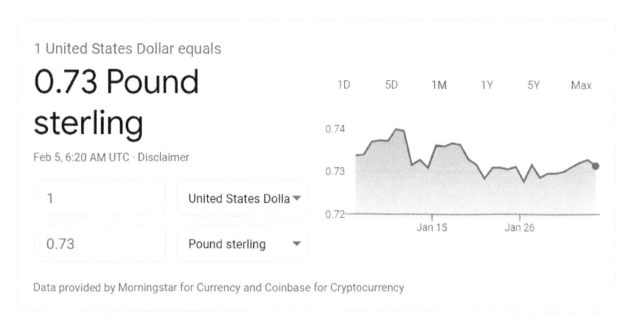

1 United States Dollar equals

0.73 Pound sterling

Feb 5, 6:20 AM UTC · Disclaimer

| 1 | United States Dolla ▼ |
| 0.73 | Pound sterling ▼ |

Data provided by Morningstar for Currency and Coinbase for Cryptocurrency

This means that as of February 5, 2021, the US Dollar (USD) would get you 73 cents worth of currency in Britain. For Americans, this is not beneficial because it's more expensive for us to buy goods and services since our currencies are not worth the same. The "same" would be if our 1 dollar would equal 1 pound. On the other hand, that's beneficial for those in the UK as US goods and services are cheaper because their pound would exchange into more US dollars, allowing them to buy more.

Once you have that tool open, you can type in the pound sterling box the amount that you'd like to have in spending money, and it'll tell you how much USD you need to reach that number of pounds.

Alternatively, say you've been spending money while abroad in an unfamiliar currency and you want to know how much you have left in UDS, you can Google "Currency X to USD".

We'll talk about how to do quick mental conversions in your head while you're abroad later in this section.

How much cash you'll need

It's never a good idea to wander around with huge amounts of cash on you in any currency, but there's also plenty of situations that could get you in a pickle if you have none at all. It's all about figuring that happy medium for your trip. There's factors to consider when deciding how much you should get, but it largely depends on what you plan to do.

Will you be tipping a lot?
Will you be buying from small shops (carts, food trucks, huts, etc) that aren't as likely to have card readers?
Will you be bar hopping?

Those are some good reasons to get out a few hundred in cash for a one week trip, but you should have the option to use a card more often than not, except in very remote areas. So, the more you plan to use cash to pay for smaller transactions, the more cash you should order. The more you plan to use your card, the less cash. Find your happy medium for your activities and how long you're traveling for.

Ordering or getting cash

There are plenty of ways of getting cash, some ways just have more of a fee to pay. Shop around for the best options for you, here are some of the most common ones:

ATMs
Automated Teller Machines (yes, it's silly to say ATM Machine) are great and pretty abundant while traveling. Typically anyone can use an ATM with any bank that's supported by VISA or Mastercard. You'll be able to put your card in, enter your pin, and withdraw money (if you've told your bank you're traveling, more on that in a bit). You might be charged what's called a "foreign transaction fee" for using an ATM that doesn't belong to your bank. "Foreign" in this case doesn't mean non-US, it just means any machine that's not owned by your bank.

THERE IS A DIFFERENCE BETWEEN DEBIT AND CREDIT CARDS. Credit cards are not intended for ATM use, debit cards are. The reason why is pretty simple, debit cards are the gateway to the money that's actually in your account. It's yours to turn into cash. Credit cards are "lines of credit", meaning it's a form of money, sure, but it's an advance from the bank, it's not actual cash. You're borrowing it until you pay it back. When you try to get cash using a credit card, it's called a cash advance and it's much riskier for banks since they don't have the guarantee you'll pay it back, therefore it usually comes with waaay higher fees. I don't recommend using a credit card for cash advances. Plus the ATM will likely ask for a PIN Number that you might not know or have set up.

Ordering currencies at your bank or credit union
Most banks have the option available to order other currencies for you. Sometimes this method can be cheaper as banks have more buying power than we do as individuals, but it's still important to shop around for rates. You can compare the rates and fees at different banks or credit unions, but you'll likely have to have an active account in order for them to issue the purchase for you. Each bank and credit union have their policies on if you can order over the phone, online, or in person, as well as their fees so just call and ask your local branch for more information. Exchange rates are constantly fluctuating, which is out of the bank's control, however, the fees and rate that they charge you for ordering the currency are within their control but not likely to be altered.

You'll have to decide how much you're looking to exchange and in what denominations. You can ask about the rate before deciding and they should be able to calculate the numbers for you on how much your home currency will be in the other currency and tweak accordingly.

Once you decide how much you want, you need to specify what denominations (which bills) you want, I recommend having a 60/40 rule. I'd recommend 60% of your bills to be the equivalent of $10 and under so you can make easy purchases and pay for services (taxi, tuk-tuks, quick snacks, tipping, etc). And the other 40% can be in a bit larger bills to pay for bigger items like meals, accommodations or longer transportation trips, etc.

The teller should provide a receipt of the transaction and let you know the details of how and when the money will arrive. Typically it's only a few days and they'll call your number on file to let you know when the money is available for pick up. Once you pick it up or it's shipped to you, you'll have an envelope of cash!

Airport
You can also go through a similar translation as with the bank while you're at the airport, there will almost always be an exchange kiosk or counter for exchanging currencies. There will be tons of options at larger airports, so look around or ask what the fees are before deciding. Airports are usually not the cheapest place that you can find to exchange money as their rates are probably a bit higher. However, you can decide if that convenience or necessity is worth that cost. You need to decide how much and specify what denominations, the same rules apply. It is possible that these providers might be short of specific denominations as they are constantly exchanging and someone might have already wiped them out of a certain bill.

Where to Keep your cash

Do not keep all of your cash in one place. Split it up among your belongings in case you get robbed or lose your purse, wallet, piece of luggage. It's best to pick 2 or 3 spots to store your cash that's not easily noticed but you won't forget where you put it. That's a panic attack waiting to happen, trust me.

For the cash that you keep on you, I'd recommend having an estimation of what you'll likely spend that day and then add a bit more, just in case. Keep a bill of the lowest denomination on the outside to make yourself less of a target for attentive pickpockets. (Don't keep your wallet in your back pocket or leave your purse on the back of chairs). Try not to flash cash around unnecessarily. Pay in bills that make sense for the purchase, it's not always easy to have options to break big bills, so plan accordingly.

Using your card

Like I said at the beginning of this section, your card will be accepted most places. More and more businesses are getting the technology to accept cards, even small vendors like food trucks and beach side shanties. While it's still a good idea to have a little bit of cash, you can mostly bank on using your card if it's VISA and Mastercard. Other card networks might be accepted, but it's not nearly as reliable.

You can find out what network your card uses by looking for the symbol on the card itself. The location varies a lot on cards, but mine are usually on the bottom right corner. Look for the big four: Visa, Mastercard, Discover, and American Express (AmEx). It's typically a logo, not just small words.

What's a card network, you ask? Well in layman's terms, it's the 'thing" that that machine uses to ask your card issuer (your bank) if you have the funds available and make sure that your card isn't marked for fraud. It's essentially the technology that checks if you have the money or not, and will tell the machine (the place you're trying to shop at) whether the transaction is approved or denied. VISA and Mastercard are the most widely accepted/used networks that machines use. So if you try to use a American Express, for example, there's a chance the machine won't be able to speak that language, so to speak. Same thing for Discover.

While I wouldn't recommend getting cards that use Discover or American Express, it doesn't mean that they can't be used. Some machines will accept them, but while you're abroad especially, I would rather you be safe and have at least one card that uses Mastercard or VISA.

I mentioned previously the difference between debit and credit cards. If you're a credit card holder who puts most of your transactions on it to get the rewards like I do, then I would recommend that you also carry a debit card. Just in case one of your cards doesn't work, you have a backup to try and the debit card provides more options to get cash out if you need to. I personally don't use my debit card often, especially when I'm traveling abroad, but it gives me a bit of peace of mind knowing that I have it with me.

Letting your bank know you're traveling
Not sure if you know this, but most banks have got your back! Their systems flag suspicious behavior (high volume purchases, purchases made far away, etc) and they can suspend the transaction until it's confirmed that you're the one who made the purchase. Some banks will text you and you can reply "yes or no" to confirm or deny that the expense was fraudulent. Some banks will just freeze your card until you talk to a representative. It's a good practice to call your bank or talk to a teller to put "travel notes" on your account. This just means that you're telling your bank that you're going to X location and to let the transactions go through because it is you.

The process of letting them know is pretty simple, you call your bank and they can transfer you to the appropriate line or you call the automated number on the back of your card. Tell them you want to put travel notes on your card (it might be an automated system that repeats everything back to you). They'll need to know where you're going (countries) and the dates you'll be there. Have your card or account number ready, they'll probably need a few forms of verification that it's your account. And that's it. You're good to go, should have no issues. No further action needed. Takes about 3-10 minutes.

An exception to this is travel cards. Credit Cards that are designed for travel use should never require you to do this step and they also usually don't have any foreign transaction fees.

<u>Tipping</u>
Some countries don't have tipping as part of their culture, instead they either bake it into what they charge you or just take it as an insult. Here's a pretty good article about <u>tipping norms around the world.</u>

Rule of thumbs for conversions
Onto the tough part for most of us: Math.

One thing that I feel like affects me more in terms of culture shock when I go somewhere unfamiliar is not knowing what something is worth in terms of my dollar. It's hard to look at prices of items when you don't know if 1000 Rupees is cheap, expensive, average, or outrageous. You need a way to get a general idea of what the destination currency is compared to your home currency.

Luckily there are usually little shortcuts you can use as guidelines. My standard practice is to look for how much five dollars and twenty dollars are worth in the destination currency. That allows me to estimate most of what I'm looking to purchase to decide if it's worth it for me. I chose five and twenty because five is small enough to be relevant to the ice cream, drink, snack, or ticket entry prices I'm usually looking at and twenty can help me figure out the bigger items like bigger meals, accommodations, or more expensive activities.

Here's a conversation I might have with myself about converting prices:

"Oh that shake looks super yummy! How much is it?
It's 25 Croatian Kunas. Okay, so I know that 31 kunas = 5 dollars (as of Feb 2021), so the price of 25 is less than 31, so it's less than 5 dollars.

Great! I'd pay that, I'm going to get it. "

Now here's another conversation I might have with myself for bigger ticket items:

"Ooooo! Look! There's a wine and dinner tour for the evening for 370 Croatian Kunas.

Okay, I know that 20 dollars is about 125 Kunas, so 125+125 is 250, that's 40. If I add another 125 then it's 375, so that's just under 60 dollars.

Mmm, that's a bit expensive for my budget right now, maybe it's not worth it. I can just get wine at this cute restaurant up the road. "

I know math can be hard to keep straight in your mind, especially when you're already overwhelmed by all the new sights, smells, and sounds, but it's a skill that gets better with practice. You can find the rule of thumb that works best for you, just know that there are little tricks you can memorize as you get the hang of it. You'll be able to judge prices more quickly the longer you're there, probably without you even realising the progress you're making! #LittleVictories

There's also always technology to help, but I'd say at least give it a shot to try the mental math first for the little items. It gets old to always have to google the conversion, but it is certainly an option.

Fun Fact: For those of you who didn't grow up less than 2 hours away from the Canadian border like me, fun fact is that Canada's currency is also called the Dollar ($). Their symbol is CAD (the US dollar is USD) so if you ever order something from Canada and it says the total price is $ 45 CAD, it's telling you that it's Canadian dollars, not US dollars, so the price is actually going to be different than the US Dollar price.

Some currencies will be closer to your home currency so it'll be easier to just know that something is relatively close in price, just a bit more expensive or cheaper. So sticking with my theme there, the Canadian Dollar is typically fairly close to the US dollar in value, so our prices often look more similar. The same conversion tricks apply, you just need to establish a baseline of your choosing to compare. "Okay, I know 75 Canadian dollars comes out to about 60 US Dollars, so since this is 60 Canadian, it'll at least be less than 60 US."

Sales Tax Vs. VAT

Have you ever heard of something called VAT? Probably not if you haven't made it to Europe yet.

So in the US, we have sales taxes. Each state can decide what their sales tax percentage is. In Texas it's 6.25%, Colorado it's 2.9%, California 7.25%, and so on. Alaska, Delaware, Montana, New Hampshire and Oregon don't have a sales tax. So when you buy most goods and/or services from a business in the states that have a sales tax, the item might be worth $1, but you will pay $1.06 for example. To put things simply, it's a way for the state to collect money for state and local budget items like schools, roads and fire departments.

In over 160 other countries, including all of Europe, they use a Value-Added Tax (VAT) system instead. I'll keep things simple and just say the benefit of this method is in place to prevent double taxation.

I'm going to over simplify how it works by just saying that the tax is calculated at each stage of manufacturing and therefore "baked into" the cost. That just means that the tax is already included, the whole process typically results in crisp, even numbers unlike in the US where we have to pay those additional cents. This allows you to be able to pay for items using the awesome 1 or 2 euro coins without getting a bunch of change back. Pretty great if you ask me.

TIME CHANGES

There's not many things to say other than just the fact that you need to be aware of them, especially when calculating your plans for transportation or check in. To find out what time zone a city or country is in while you're planning, just google it. There are some apps available to show you the time zones if you're traveling great distances.

It's important to note that your arrival time listed on flights or other transportation will be in the time zone that you arrive in, not the time zone that you're coming from. There won't be a need to convert anything. But, with that said, pay attention to when that time is because trains, shuttles, boat schedules usually end at a certain time and you'll need transportation from the airport to your destination.

Example: Your flight leaves in the evening Chicago time and you arrive in Kyoto, Japan at 4am. The trains might not be running to take you downtown to your hostel until 6am. There might be ubers, but that could cost up to $150.

Also be mindful of your check in times. I got off the train I took from Lisbon to Madrid at 7:20am and I couldn't check into my hostel until 10am, so I had to haul my pack until that time when usually I would go straight to the hostel to lock up my bag then go exploring without it. It's not the end of the world, just keep it in mind when planning, ESPECIALLY when arriving late at night.

PHONE SERVICES

Ahhh, the all in one device that I don't know what I would do without. My phone is basically my lifeline when traveling but I've never actually paid for an international phone plan.

So, long story short is that using your phone abroad is not usually included in your phone plan and using it abroad usually comes with added fees. The fees themselves depend on your network provider (AT&T, Verizon, T Mobile, etc) and the plan that you buy.

You have some options to use your phone while you're out of the country:
- Don't use data or messaging, just use WIFI
- Sign up for a travel plan with your network
- Buy or rent a wifi hotspot (great for remote traveling, I used one around Iceland)
- Get a international SIM card to use in your unlocked phone
- For long term, you can buy a phone in your destination country

There are pros and cons to each option, so you'll have to decide what's best for you.

Personally, I'm usually fine with just using WIFI where I can find it. I'm a Type A planner, so I usually have most of what I need already researched or downloaded. Waiting for WIFI might not be a great situation for someone who likes to look things up in the moment, so upgrading to a limited data international plan might be the way to go. Usually you can just extend to that plan for a certain amount of time and then downgrade back to your normal domestic plan.

Most plans nowadays in the US allow for some messaging and calling to be free to Canada and Mexico but data is often still charged at higher rates.

A SIM (Subscriber Identity Module) card is a small plastic card that goes inside any phone that uses the Global System of Mobile Communications (GSM, for short).
I've had some friends try the international SIM card route, some with success and others thought it wasn't worthwhile but it's not too expensive to try as SIM cards are usually under $40. It's more geared towards those who are staying for longer stretches of time like a semester abroad or there for work. You'll likely still have to pay for a phone plan, but it's likely to be cheaper than the abroad fees of your US provider over time.

My general advice would be to look at what plans or deals your current provider offers and move down the list of options from there. For short trips, paying whatever your provider offers is likely to be the most convenient option with the least amount of logistics to figure out. Just be sure that you understand the plan you're agreeing to so you don't accidentally go beyond it and get slapped with fees.

The most important advice I have about phones is to TURN OFF YOUR MOBILE DATA when you aren't actively trying to use it. Your phone apps will be searching, updating, running in the background using up your data without you knowing. The best way to protect yourself from fees or charges is to just turn off the mobile data all together. That setting is in your settings or likely on among your options when you swipe for your notification panel.

Airplane mode is also helpful for when you want to save battery because it disables the phone from searching for networks. Some phones will also allow you to set notifications to alert you when you use a certain amount of data and also set a limit that you can't pass, I've found those to be extremely useful just to get an idea of what I use normally.

Useful apps to have downloaded

- Google Maps
  - You can download certain regions or cities to work while offline (no data or wifi)
- Facebook Messenger
  - Communicate for free on wifi, easy way to send pictures, keep in touch
- Whatsapp
  - Used worldwide for international friends, more common to connect on here with people you meet around the world.
- Airbnb
- HostelWorld
- AllTrails
  - For hiking and exploring the wilderness
- World Clock
  - Apps available to help you keep track of what time it is in certain regions as you travel
- Google Translate with download option
  - Download certain languages to be able to search while offline.
- Airline App that you're flying with
  - Makes boarding and navigating the airport easier
- Ride Sharing apps
  - Uber, Lyft, etc
- Entertainment
  - Audible, Netflix, Amazon Video, Hulu, Disney+, etc all have download options
- Music
  - Spotify, Pandora, Apple Music, etc

Not only do you have to realise what you'd regret if you do, but also if you don't.

SAFETY

You don't need me to tell you to be safe. Your loved ones will probably say it enough times. What I want to offer you are steps you can take to prepare and protect yourself. There are quite a few actions you can take before you go.

Learn where the bad neighborhoods are

DISCLAIMER: This is not a fool proof method and it is based on a ton of assumptions, not all areas will be accurately assessed. You might misjudge an area, but so what? We're talking about your safety here. I'm a petite young woman that tends to stick out, so I tend to use more caution than not. I'm okay with the fact that I could miss out on what *might* turn out to be a cool area based on my misjudgement. If you get bad vibes from an area, then avoid it. Simple as that. Spend the extra $10 dollars if you need to/can. Safety is paramount.

This one is a good place to start as you're doing research on where you want to go and stay anyways. Sometimes it's pretty easy to find out, start with the top of the list and if that doesn't prove to be helpful, then move down the line.

1. Google "unsafe neighborhoods in ___" or "Safest area for tourists in ____" to get started.
   - Read the forums, comments, and articles that come up. Keep in mind how old they are. Look for anything within 5 years. A lot can change in 10 years that might not be relevant at all anymore, but typically within 5 years is worth seriously considering. Reviews are super helpful.
2. Look for trends in pricing of accommodations. One cheap room doesn't mean it's a bad area, but typically if there's a cluster of suuuuuper cheap options compared to the rest of the listings, then it might be a bad neighborhood.
   - Look for the listings descriptions. A lot of the time it'll say blankly "In a safe neighborhood" "safe for walking to the bus station" "low crime area" or something of the sort.
   - In my experience, not a lot of people falsely claim to be in a safe area when they're not. If they don't mention anything at all, maybe consider going with a listing that does make that claim.
3. Use the street view of Google Maps.
   - Put in the address of the accommodation you're looking at into Google Maps and pull the little yellow man into the streets. Click around for a minute to see the state of the area. Tons of graffiti, trash, and broken windows is probably a sign you don't want to be there, not walking around at night at least. If you don't have an address, then just pluck the little man anywhere.

Someone else having your itinerary or location

An easy way you can give yourself and those who care about you a little comfort is to share your itinerary with at least 2 people. You don't have to share every detail, but a general outline of your plans should be sufficient. I also recommend sharing your location with a couple people so they can keep an eye on you if needed. Google maps makes it easy among other apps, some I'll mention below specifically about safety.

When you're out at night walking or in a less than safe situation, text or call a loved one, tell them that you're out and about, where you're headed, and approximately how long it should take you to get there. You could also throw in your general route. It costs nothing and is easy to do. You have to let them know when you get there safely though, or they'll worry. Communication is key here.

Blending In and being aware

Blending in with the crowd may sound lame, but it's a good thing to not draw negative attention to yourself, especially at night. You don't want to end up as someone sinister's next target. When I say blend in, I don't mean your outfit (what we wear shouldn't determine if we should be respected). What I mean is don't act like you're the clueless tourist that clearly doesn't have anyone around to call for help. Blend in like a local, don't draw attention to yourself, don't be obnoxious and loud, don't act like a drunk idiot. Don't have both earbuds blaring music while looking down at your phone when walking at night. You might get away with it in the day, although still not a great idea when you're around roads.

Be.aware.of.your.surroundings. I cannot stress this enough.

It costs you nothing to have an eye on who is around you, where you're going, and what you're passing on the way to your destination. It could cost a lot more if you don't. I'm not trying to be scary, but the reality is that it's a scary world. Being alert is your first defense. Being alert gives you the opportunity to see what might be coming if you're attacked, might give you a chance to see identifying features on someone, might make you less of a target for someone up to no good. Just be careful, okay?

Self protection moves

If being alert is the first line of defense you have, learning some protection moves is the second. Take a page out of Miss Congeniality and learn how to SING. It's a scene about how women can do major damage to an attacker in 4 key ways. Slamming force into 4 body parts: solarplex (guts), instep (foot), nose, and groin.

Watch the clip here: https://www.youtube.com/watch?v=ZNJwxJXr2jc

Watch some more self defense videos for women here:
https://www.youtube.com/watch?v=KVpxP3ZZtAc
https://www.youtube.com/watch?v=Ww1DeUSC94o

I know that watching videos is one thing and performing these moves is another, but at least arm yourself with the basic knowledge of how these moves work. It'd be awesome if we all took some self defense lessons, but at least start here.

Taking it a step further would be to ask someone in your life to run some drills with you. Women, I would recommend asking someone to practice the motions in slow-mo with you a few times each, just for some "experience". No need to actually do damage (on purpose at least), but it's beneficial to get the feeling of it.

I've asked a couple of different males over the last few years and they've always been more than willing to work with me. Muscle memory can be much more reliable than our brains can be when you need to spring into action immediately.

Some other self defense tips:
- Try to leave a scratch

- Go for the eyes
- Look for tattoos (for reporting purposes)
- Try to note general weight and height if you can (for reporting purposes)
- Be as loud as possible
- Carry a personal alarm (you activate it and an intense siren goes off to attract attention when in danger or hopefully thwart an attack.
    - https://www.alarmnewengland.com/blog/best-personal-alarms

Apps for safety

For traveling in the US:
Here's an article on some options.

I like Noonlight and bSafe. Noonlight is a button you hold down when you feel unsafe. Once you're safe, you release it and put in your 4 digit pin. If you don't put in your pin (aka, something happens to you) it alerts the police and sends your location.

bSafe can be voice activated and alerts your guardians or set contacts, also begins to record audio and video and streams it directly to your set contacts.

For traveling in the US:
There's an app called Red Panic Button. Once you set it up, it's a button you can push on your phone to automatically send emergency messages to your emergency contacts in different ways (SMS, email, etc) that includes your latest location.
Do a quick google search of apps that might fit your needs. Chances are there's one out there.

STEP program
The US has a free service to all US citizens that enrolls your trip with the nearest US Embassy to you. It's called the Smart Traveler Enrollment Program. This program is cool for a few reasons. One, it's free. Two, once you set it up, you can login in to update your trips/addresses abroad. Three, it might make your family feel a little more at ease when you're traveling.

Here's how it works:
Fill out the from online. You're providing your contact information to the nearest embassies around where you're traveling. They'll be able to send you updates on safety concerns or crises and be quicker to help you in case of a medical, legal or financial emergency. You'll still need to have forms of ID, though. (aka passport).

It takes about 15 minutes, check it out. It made my parents feel better. Also FYI, Every time your passport is scanned, it's logged, so there's a kind of passport paper trail of your location.

<u>Closing notes on safety</u>

I say all this only to prepare you for what could impact you when you're traveling, but the reality, you should keep these in mind for anytime. I could argue that my hometown has more crime per capita in the surrounding 30 mile radius than most of the places that I've traveled to. I feel the need to be on guard in more situations when I'm doing my normal life activities at home than I do a lot of times abroad. Unfortunately, there are people out there with some sinister intentions and they don't care whether you're going grocery shopping or on vacation, so please be aware of your surroundings and take what measures you can to protect yourself no matter the situation. With that said...

Remember that the people that care about you are going to worry while you're traveling. You being far away from the comforts and safety of home is really hard on some parents or loved ones, so be gentle and reassuring with them, but hold your ground and let them know what steps you're taking to be proactive and prepared. There's no price to peace of mind, and there's a huge cost to constant worry. Be thankful for the love that you have in your life and appreciate that they care what happens to you, even when parents, significant others, and friends might pester you.

WHAT TO PACK

Drum roll please....IT'S TIME TO PACK. I bet you have an itch right now to start thinking about or actually grabbing the clothes that you want to take right now, don't you? It's exciting! It's fun to imagine what we'll wear and how many cute pics we'll take. So without further ado...

Let's start with general tips and guidelines.

- **Layers are your best bet. Always.** Having options is always helpful, but you're only going to have so much space. So look for options that can be comfortably put on top of each other. A giant heavy sweater might be great outside in Iceland but you might be dying from overheating in the car. Your cute light sundress might be sooo fetch (#MeanGirlsReference), but you might be freezing when you're in the restaurant. Layers give you the opportunity to adjust throughout the multiple environments you'll be in throughout the day.

- **Less is more.** Every serious traveller will preach this to you: Do not overpack. Take only what you'll actually wear and no more. Wear things more than once. You will literally have to haul or carry all of your items so keep it light. It's so much easier to get around, as well as decide what to wear, when you have your set favs with you and no distractions from those. You do not need 7 day outfits for a 4 day trip. You do not need a full sized suitcase for a week.

- **Stick with a color palate.** Having clothes that all fit into a general color range will help so much to make the most out of the limited outfits you have to choose from because you'll be better able to mix and match. Layering comes back into play here because when everything goes well together, you have more variety to make different outfits out of the same items. I love earth tones and earth tones look great on me, so #winwin

- **Practical and comfortable will get you further.** Yes it's so fun to think about wearing that outfit that you never get a chance to wear, but do you never get the chance, or is it just not that comfortable to wear all day? Wearing shorts that rub wrong, a dress that makes you self conscious, a shirt that won't stay down, or shoes that hurt will not add value to your trip because they were cute. They'll make you uncomfortable and maybe give you chub rub (your legs rubbing together) or blisters. Focus more on the experiences you'll have than what you will look like. Stick with your regulars that fit well and you feel comfortable in. You wear them more in your normal life for a reason. This especially applies to shoes - cute but no support will just make you miserable for no reason. There's plenty of cute shoes that will work, just skip the heels or flat little sandals or flip flops on the walking days.

- **Brand new is not a good idea.** I'm not talking about getting new items while you're on your trip, shop away my friend, within reason. What I'm talking about is don't take something with you that you've never worn before. Take it for a test drive to see how it fits and how you feel in it doing actual activities. Wear it around the house for a few hours. Wear it to do errands. ESPECIALLY with shoes. Always break in your shoes before you go to avoid the pain while you're exploring.

- **Try to keep it simple.** Having blatant Americana clothing might make you look extra touristy. High school sport team tees might stick out. Try to avoid most things branded with religion, profane, or USA. It makes mix and matching easier too. Soccer jerseys though, 10/10 common in tons of countries.

- **Take what you packed, cut out at least 5 items.** I'm serious. No joke, friend. You probably will still overpack, so once you're "done", take some away. Think about the actual days you've planned. Does that outfit still seem necessary? Do you need 3 sets of pajama bottoms? Will you actually go to a 5 star restaurant? Does that second cardigan match everything? Take stuff out pal, you'll be fine without it. Maybe it'll give you a chance to shop for something new if you actually do need it while you're there. Start with cutting out any of the "maybe I'll need this" items. I still have to check myself on this.

- **Jeans are classic for a reason, but be mindful of them in hot or rainy climates.** They take forever to dry and get really uncomfortable and are heavy when wet. Pack more options.

- **Always have some sort of jacket.** Going to a tropical island? Still take a jacket. Cool night breezes or heavy AC drafts might leave you shivering. Going somewhere rainy? Make it a waterproof or resistant one. Going somewhere cold? Still be able to layer.

- **Leave the flashy jewelry at home.** If it's at home, it won't make you a higher target and it'll be safer. This is more important in lower income countries especially, but good advice for traveling in general.

Remember that most things that you may need but don't have, you can find pretty easily if you forget it. A lot of travelers recommend the 20 rule: if you can get it in under 20 minutes for under 20 dollars, don't sweat if you forgot it at home. It's not worth the mental energy worrying about it.

You'll likely have some sort of access to the following wherever you go:
- General shopping
- Groceries
- Pharmacies
- Gas stations

My travel Items that I love

Here's a list of the items that I travel with all the time. Please note that I did a lot of research when deciding on these because they were the best fit for me, and I love them. But they may not be the best match for you, so use this list as a guide and not as a must have. Click around and think about your specific needs. Especially when it comes to hiking boots and backpack.

Visit Collectingthepostcards.com for the links!

- ❐ TravelWise Packing Cubes - 3 Piece Set
- ❐ Universal Travel Adapter
- ❐ Phone charging cell
- ❐ Osprey Fairview 55 Women's Travel Backpack
- ❐ Waterproof Backpack cover
- ❐ Microfiber Towels - Quick Dry 3 Size Pack
- ❐ Mini luggage lock
- ❐ Wool socks
- ❐ Columbia hiking boots - waterproof is awesome! Many options, I wanted ankle support.
- ❐ Solid liquids bag - not a must have, but nice if you travel frequently. Ziplock bag will work too.
- ❐ Travel Money Belt - not a must have, but helpful to have in sketchy areas.
- ❐ Fast drying water shoes - not a must for all trips but great for beaches and nature exploring

Picking out a hiking backpack

First of all, whether you're hiking in the mountains or backpacking across cities in Europe, hiking packs are the BEST. Yes you have to carry it, but they're super comfortable to let you walk so much more comfortably and faster than hauling a suitcase on wheels around. Europe is covered in cobblestone, people, it's a loud nightmare.

I didn't get this until after a few trips and I wish I would have sooner. If you plan on moving from spot to spot while you travel, it's worth the money.

There are tons of articles out there to read about the factors to consider, but here were my main points. I don't have any affiliate links, but Osprey is definitely the way to go in my mind. Just my opinion though. Read through the reviews to find people who have commented on their experience that have similar body types as you (weight and heights) to find the best fit.

- **Fit / comfortability.** I needed something to fit my narrow frame, which led me to the Fairview option built for women's frames.
- **Carry on size.** 55L is around the size that airplanes still allow on as a carry on. I checked the dimensions to make sure and I've never had an issue once in the probably 30 flights that I've taken that bag on. It fits in the overhead compartments just fine.
- **Dual bags.** I wanted something that held a lot of stuff but gave me the option of the day bag when I didn't need to carry around the huge bag. It's been great! The smaller bag zips onto the larger one so it stays snug and doesn't flop around on me. I've loved having that option.
- **Full zipper open.** Some bags are designed to only open from the top, so you have to take out EVERYTHING in order to reach something at the bottom. This upside down U shaped design lets me unzip to the bottom of the bag to grab stuff without taking everything out. It's been a blessing more times than I can count.
- **Water bottle sleeve.** Simple enough, I wanted something to hold my bottle so I didn't have to carry it or shove it in my bag all the time. Not all packs come with this option though, so don't forget to look!
- **Hip support.** Most "serious" hiking backpacks have the hip support that buckles around your hips. It takes such a load off of your back, literally. It's so comfy to wear and I like the grounded feeling it gives me, like I'm in control of at least one thing in this crazy world. My bag is strapped onto me and it's not going anywhere.

I love my backpack like it's a friend. We've been through so much together and it's always had (been on) my back. <3

Another important note is to lock your bag! I know sometimes it will feel like overkill, but when you're in cities especially, it's a good idea. **Use one of the luggage locks** with a simple code to better secure your stuff, plus it's a deterrent for pickpockets to skip over you and go for an easier target. I'd definitely recommend using one with a code and not a key because those keys are so tiny and easy to lose.

If you're looking for more of a normal everyday backpack, I'd just recommend looking for ones with a water bottle side pocket, a smaller front pocket, and cushioned straps. But to each their own! I've traveled with my school backpack on two separate week long Europe trips and it was great. You don't need to shell out a bunch of money to travel semi-comfortably.

Quick note on packing cubes:

Not worth it if you're only taking a trip or two, but totally worth it if you travel a lot. It's so nice to be able to open my back and not have undies fall out in the airport. Peace of mind is important, haha. It makes getting a specific thing out easier for me because I know which cube I put it in. If it's not in a cube, I can just take the cubes out to grab the item then shove the cubes back in the bag and we're on our way again.

FINAL THOUGHTS

I don't even know what to say! I hope that this book helps you along your journeys and that you find immeasurable amounts of joy in your adventures. I like the idea of ending on a high note of inspiration, so here are some final quotes that get my wanderlust sparking.

If you change the way you look at things, the things you look at change.

One day you will thank yourself for never giving up

"How long are you going to wait before you demand the best for yourself?"
- Epictetus

"Just when you think it can't get any worse, it can. And just when you think it can't get any better, it can."
— Nicholas Sparks

"If you can't change your fate, change your attitude."
— Amy Tan

"At one point in your life you either have the thing you want or the reasons why you don't."
— Andy Roddick

Keep calm and Travel on.

Printed in Great Britain
by Amazon